Sacré-Cœur et Montmartre

Rive Droite

Le Marais

Louvre

Notre Dame

Île Saint-Louis

Place de la Bastille

Place Saint-Sulpice

La Seine

Jardin des Plantes

Teatime in Paris!

To Mum and Dad

For stopping off at that first

French pâtisserie...

Teatime in Paris!

A WALK THROUGH EASY FRENCH PÂTISSERIE RECIPES

Jill Colonna

WAVERLEY
BOOKS

Contents

Picture opposite: Chocolate-hazelnut financiers topped with light coffee cream

INTRODUCTION
Demystifying Parisian Pastry

Recreate the exquisite styles and tastes of French pâtisserie in your own home

I can't help it. I've tried to curb my inner excitement, but each time I aim for a Parisian museum, an art gallery, or any fashion store for that matter, I'm invariably drawn instead to one of the many high-end pâtisseries that are on the rise around the City of Light. They're my kind of gallery. They just ooze sweet inspiration.

With every visit I never fail to be bowled over. I have the highest respect for the delicate precision and *savoir-faire* of these pastry chefs and chocolate makers. Unlike myself, they have patience, and their talent and training culminates in the most gorgeous, scrumptious works of art.

Their delicious creations, balanced to perfection with intriguing flavours, are sweet memories in the making. Such masterpieces often look too good to eat but, most important to the French, the height of pleasure is their lasting exquisite taste.

As much as we admire their stunning pâtisserie, it's easy to be put off trying to make it. French pâtisserie looks fiddly and time-consuming. Even some of my French friends think making éclairs, religieuses, macarons or tartlets must be hard.

The truth is, with some basic techniques and such inspiring ideas at our disposal, it's possible to recreate our own inexpensive versions at home.

If you can make a batch of cookies, muffins, pancakes or scones, you can make French pâtisserie.

Having been there myself, I have tried to demystify the art of pâtisserie in this book. It is structured starting with the quickest and easiest little cakes, then walks step-by-step through a comprehensive series of pâtisserie recipes to the slightly more technical ones. We finish with the *crème de la crème*: afternoon treats for special occasions where you can have fun mixing and matching all the previous sections' recipes.

Most recipes are presented within their historical context, because many French treats have fascinating stories behind them. As many boutiques have their particular specialities, I've also added key tasting streets around the city – where you can sample some of the best pastries of that kind in Paris.

Finally, at the end of this book, jump on the metro, bus or water taxi and stop at the likes of the Eiffel Tower, Saint Germain-des-Prés or Le Marais and join me on a treasure hunt, popping in to many of my favourite pâtisseries along the way.

So – are you ready for our pastry-walk through Paris, step by step? Let's get the aprons on, crack some eggs together and bring a light Parisian touch to teatime.

Picture opposite: Crumble top choux puff with vanilla pasty cream, see pages 63, 70 and 72

HOW THE FRENCH EAT PASTRY
Yet Can Stay Slim

The French traditionally know how to look after their silhouettes. It's no secret and yet so simple: they don't snack or graze throughout the day, but rather stick to regular mealtimes at the table. When it comes, however, to quatre heures – *4 o'clock* goûter *or teatime – it's considered as an official treat to tide you over until dinner later in the evening.*

If twenty years ago a psychic had revealed that today I'd have a bilingual French–Scottish family, be obsessed about enjoying and taking my time eating good food, even revelling in sweet treats made with cream, butter and sugar, I would have asked for my money back.

You see, when I naïvely landed in Paris in January 1993, it was a continuing student adventure: I had no idea if it was a one-way ticket or just an attempt to learn French in a couple of months before returning to a real marketing job in Scotland.

The only thing I had was a suitcase of shoulder-padded sweaters and a cliché of having gone weak at the knees in love. I had followed a Frenchman with a sexy accent to Paris. At first I felt like a tourist … until reality set in, with a thud as depressing as my limited cooking experience.

My dull menu options stemmed from a long-guarded secret: I was obsessed about my weight – at one point even considered anorexic, and on a constant, miserable diet. How on earth could I have considered food as just plain, uninteresting fuel? How could I have denied myself such great taste experiences and flavours?

Picture opposite: Saint Honoré, see page 199

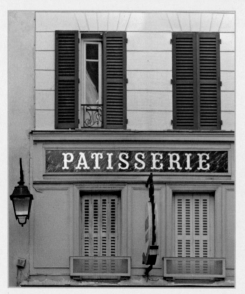

As a vegetarian, an apple-and-cheese girl, I made Antoine, my French husband-to-be, nervous, as he contemplated my mundane sweet proposals, from "What about an orange?" to "Banana Surprise?" (banana slices hidden under a fluorescent dollop of custard from a packet mix). Cringing in front of our polite yet silently horrified French guests (Antoine's French friends and Corsican family), the quickest – and most expensive – solution was to run to the nearest chic pâtisserie.

Yet why was I putting on weight suddenly while most French ladies around me remained slim? The only part of me that was actually losing weight was my purse. How could they indulge in an afternoon pastry? It wasn't fair being smitten with the sweet life.

Antoine's sobering advice was infuriatingly basic and yet so fundamentally French: "We don't snack; we stick to regular mealtimes and eat at the table."

It's that easy? I didn't think so.

Today, just take a look at the traditional brasseries and bistros around the business areas of Paris (rather than the tourist spots that serve 24/7): the tables are cleared and emptied before 3 o'clock. Generally speaking, the French don't eat at any old time of day. They take pride in sitting down to eat at mealtimes; you won't find many French people carrying coffees and eating while on the move in the street – although sadly this is rapidly changing with the younger generation. No, they take their time to appreciate what they're eating and enjoy passionate conversation around it at the table.

Thankfully I landed a job to help with the shop-bought pastry budget. I lunched and learned from my new elegant French girlfriends.

Double Chocolate Tartlet, see page 113

It was time to adapt previous eating habits to theirs. They regularly chose a light, salad-style lunch and refused the dessert menu. Instead, they'd often buy a light treat from a pâtisserie on the way back to the office. Their secret was to patiently wait for the sweet prize and, like Antoine, if they occasionally missed having lunch on time, they waited (strangely, I thought then, but now I do the same) until 4 o'clock teatime. *Enfin*, I finally had an excuse to enjoy the odd light pastry or a few macarons without the guilt. It was the official "snack" of the day without snacking: afternoon *goûter* time!

By now I can hear you: but French pastry is packed with naughty sugar and butter! It's an essential part indeed, but what's so special about Parisian pâtisserie is that they're not overly sweet – and certainly not as sweet as the ones you find in supermarkets or more commercial bakery chains. Over the years, as my family has been drawn to better quality, we have gradually cut

Picture opposite: Pistachio-cherry eclair, page 98

14

down on sugar, use good quality fresh ingredients (seasonal and no reduced-fat dietary products) and have limited our portion sizes; all without restricting our enjoyment.

More than twenty years on, having adopted the French way of life – living, breathing, eating and dreaming their culture and language, for better or for worse – I can happily tell you that it has been for the better. Life is healthily sweet and the cherry on the *gâteau* is when French friends and family now enjoy popping in for some light and tasty homemade Parisian surprises ... at teatime.

FRENCH PASTRY
A Step at a Time

Just following a few simple guidelines will make your journey très facile!

It's amazing how the word *pâtisserie* can sound – dare I say – rather "upper crust" or posh. I speak from experience when I say it's so easy to feel intimidated, especially when surrounded by top-notch pâtisseries and talented French friends who are either trained chefs or passionate perfectionist amateurs who continue to raise the entertaining bar. Thankfully, I've learned so much from them over the years.

I'm not a chef and don't pretend to be one. I'm a "lazy gourmet": if a recipe looks or sounds difficult, especially complex recipes with sugar temperatures to control (I hate sugar thermometers!), I tend to turn the page and leave the more complicated pastries to the professionals. As a busy working mum, my kind of French baking has to be easy, tasty, pretty and inexpensive to reproduce at home. In a nutshell, recipes should have that wow factor without much effort.

French pastry uses just four basic ingredients: flour, sugar, eggs and good quality butter. There are many pastries to go nuts over – especially with almonds and hazelnuts! What's particularly intriguing about French pastry is the perfectly balanced contrast between sweet and slightly salty.

Remember an extra pinch of good French sea salt – *fleur de sel* – in the dough adds that *je ne sais quoi* to your recipes.

French pâtisserie is like fashion: mix and match recipe elements according to season. France's most fashionable pastry chefs make the classics – but their revisited versions are anything but plain. Just to add to the endless choices, they also invent limited-edition pastries: using intriguing and unusual flavours, from garden-inspired combinations to speciality tea or herbal infusions, exotic Asian influences, and spicy concoctions to fire us up.

Exposed to this, it certainly influences your experimental side and entices you to play with your own personal favourite flavour-combinations. For example, take a basic pastry as a base, add some vanilla pastry cream and top with fresh, seasonal fruit and you have a summer tart that could be proudly sitting in a Paris pâtisserie window. Likewise, fill choux buns (cream puffs) with the same pastry cream, add some orange, a splash of Grand Marnier™ and you have "choux-laced" treats. The filling for the salted caramel macaron is delicious in a caramel *millefeuille* or choux puff, *religieuse* or éclair. Why don't you create them all?

OK – stop me! There are plenty more examples you can dream up for yourself based on these recipes and I welcome you to share yours via the website, **MadAboutMacarons.com**

So, you don't have much time to spend in the kitchen but want to try your hand? No problem; I've cut as many corners as I can to help you, retaining as much French authenticity as possible. As most recipes are easy to split up, many elements can be made in advance (even frozen).

Prepare ingredients in advance

For the best organisation, **prepare ingredients in advance**: it sounds obvious, but I didn't used to do this before and ever since I started, it's so much simpler to have it all in front of you, concentrate on the recipe and tidy up along the way.

Taste

Don't forget to **taste creams** before filling your pastries. Flavourings in the form of syrups, extracts or floral waters, can vary greatly in intensity from brand to brand so add a little amount, taste, then gradually add more if needed.

Measure in weight, and use a digital scale

Finally, pastry is precise so let's do it like the French: it's **weight rather than volume**. Years ago I used my simple supermarket measurer that indicated millilitres (ml) clearly for measuring out liquids. Little did I know that my pastry cream seemed more compact simply because I was measuring in volume rather than weight. When I eventually invested in a digital scale that also indicated ml, my volume-measured 500ml was, in fact, 470ml on the precise scale. Lesson learned: **weigh everything carefully with a digital scale**.

DIGITAL SCALES

Please don't start using this book without digital scales! 500ml of milk weighs 500g. So, to keep things easy, liquids are shown in grams throughout the book. **If you're used to ounces**, with digital scales you can simply switch the button over to grams and we're all talking the same sweet language. See page 212.

Get to know your oven

Get to know your oven before you do anything (especially for baking macarons): your oven is your best friend. A good way of understanding your oven is to check that it's doing what it says it's doing by checking with an **oven thermometer** (available in all good baking stores).

In this book the temperatures given are for a fan-assisted oven.

In a fan-assisted oven, the heat is more evenly distributed than in a conventional oven.

If you have a standard convection oven or a gas oven, just add 20°C more to the fan-oven temperatures that are indicated in the book, or allow for a longer cooking time. As a general guide, standard fan-assisted temperatures are:

- 150°–160°C (300–320°F, Gas 2–3) for macaron shells;
- 160°C (320°F, Gas 3) for sweet pastry, choux (éclairs) and tarts;
- 160°C (320°F, Gas 3) for mini cakes and mille-feuilles.

Experimentation is also key, so just keep an eye on whatever you're baking, especially if you're making it for the first time. If a cake recipe calls for 25 minutes baking time and it looks (and smells) perfectly ready at 20 minutes then take it out.

The recipes in this book were all made using a fan-assisted oven and so temperatures throughout are given for such an oven.

It doesn't matter if you don't have a fan-assisted oven. Fan-assisted ovens do cook a bit more evenly and slightly quicker than conventional convection ovens but if you don't have one you should either just add about 20°C on to the temperatures printed in the book, or just cook slightly longer than stated, or experiment a little using an oven thermometer. (Consult the table for fahrenheit equivalents.)

All ovens are different and we can't state exactly how yours is going to perform. Please get to know your oven, purchase an inexpensive oven thermometer and see if the temperature on the dial is telling the truth! Also please consult the manufacturer's instruction manual for further guidance.

For "Gas Mark" temperatures, it is assumed that if you have a gas oven that it is not fan-assisted (these are unusual and very expensive!) therefore Gas Marks are based on fan-assisted celcius temperatures in the book plus 20°C.

Celsius	Gas mark	Fahrenheit	Description
110	¼	230	Very slow
120	½	250	Very slow
130	½	270	Very slow
140	1	280	Slow
150	2	300	Slow
160	2 ½	320	Moderate
170	3	340	Moderate
180	4	360	Moderate
190	5	375	Moderately hot
200	6	400	Moderately hot
220	7	425	Hot
230	8	450	Hot
250	9	480	Very hot

Rue du Four translates as 'Oven Street'

With all that said, is it teatime yet? Let's get baking but take our time, step by step, with the basic recipes, in order to master the pastry building blocks. All the following recipes – tried and tested happily many times – are explained a step at a time with plenty of tips to help you along the way.

INGREDIENTS
Notes to Help You

Incredible tastes can be made with some store-cupboard staples

French pâtisserie may look as if it is created with outlandishly exotic ingredients but for the most part they are made from four ingredients that are probably already in your cupboard and fridge: flour, butter, sugar and eggs.

Other ingredients commonly used in French pâtisserie are also easily obtainable in your local supermarket: including milk, cream, cornflour (cornstarch), icing sugar (confectioner's sugar), chocolate and ground almonds (almond flour).

You can practise the basics of French pastry without having to go to speciality shops.

Top quality ingredients do change the taste of your pastries. It may sound obvious, but over the years when I've tried to cut costs – and try supermarket own-brands of chocolate, for example – the end result has been disappointingly not in the same taste (or texture) league.

Many of the best ingredients can be found under the same roof in the small street of **Rue Tiquetonne**, just off **Rue Montmartre**, another great ingredient street, near **Châtelet**.

For harder-to-get items, such as specific flavourings and good quality colourings, we have a stockists list on page 219. But don't be put off making an item because you can't find, for example, violet syrup or rosewater. Improvise with other flavourings you have to hand. Also, most of the items mentioned are easily available online. So if the supermarket doesn't have it an online shop will.

COLOURINGS

Powdered colouring is the best colouring to use, particularly for macarons, since it doesn't fade during baking and only a tiny amount is required as it's highly concentrated (I say a pinch which is the equivalent of a tiny heap at the tip of a knife). "Blossom tints" and "lustre dusts" are not meant for colouring macaron batter. (These can be used for painting and dusting the surface of macarons after baking for a final decorative effect.) Supermarket liquid colourings are not suitable for macarons. Food colour **pastes** are very good because they are concentrated and you need very little, but can be less reliable in terms of holding their colour during baking, depending on the brand. (Your discussions regarding the best available in your country are welcome on **facebook.com/MadAboutMacarons** and on the website **MadAboutMacarons.com**.)

FLAVOURINGS

Where possible, use **natural extracts** rather than artificial flavourings. Again, specialist retailers are your best bet for more unusual flavours but many good quality extracts can be found in the baking section of the average supermarket.

Several of the recipes in the book use **rosewater** (and **orange-blossom** water). I normally use light rosewater, with a concentration of 3% rose essence to water, and measurements in the book are based on this. Please take care which brand you buy when it comes to rose — some are very much stronger than others. And notice whether it is rosewater or rose essence/extract. Some flavourings in small bottles are very concentrated essences that contain propylene glycol and ethanol. The size of the bottle is often a clue as to how concentrated the essence is: small is usually very concentrated. Ideally choose rosewater with essence of rose no more than about 6%. If you are using a more

concentrated essence then you'll need very much less rose than stated in the recipes, only a few drops rather than spoons, and it is essential to add it slowly and taste as you go.

Some recipes call for adding flavoured **syrups**. Do remember that syrups also add sweetness to recipes, so if, for example, you decided to use rose syrup instead of rosewater to flavour a pastry filling you'd also have to reduce the sugar content of the recipe.

DAIRY

Unless specified, all recipes use **unsalted butter** and use fresh, organic produce. **Milk** is full-fat/full-cream (and not the longlife kind, but fresh), and **whipping cream** (or double cream, heavy cream) has 35–40% butterfat. For pastry lovers who need to be careful about consuming dairy products, replace cream with soya or coconut milk, and replace milk with almond milk.

American readers, please note that "sweet butter" is not necessarily unsalted butter. "Sweet" refers to the way it is churned from cream that has not been cultured. It can be salted or unsalted. Check the ingredients list on the packaging. (The other type of butter is "cultured butter". A continental European style of butter, whiter in colour than sweet butter.) Also, only use 100% butter, not whipped butter or low-fat spreads.

EGGS

Eggs are organic and medium-sized (a medium egg white weighs about 30–35g [1oz]). If you're looking to use egg whites to make macarons or financiers, then there are plenty of recipes specifically using up yolks. There is also a guide for egg white measurements at the back (page 218) should you find yourself short.

CHOCOLATE

In this book we'll be using good quality cooking chocolate (preferably with **couverture** written on the label), which contains natural **cocoa butter** rather than other fats, making it ideal for melting – **at least 60% cocoa solids** for dark chocolate (US: bittersweet or semisweet) and **at least 30%** for milk chocolate. I like Valhrona's baking chocolate (particularly 66% Caribbean dark chocolate) available from speciality stores. See Stockists, page 219. Otherwise you'll find baking chocolate in the baking section of most good supermarkets (I like Green & Black's in the UK and from the French supermarket I recommend the Nestlé Corsé brand). Just be careful to avoid confectionary chocolate which contains vegetable fats.

COFFEE

There are several mentions of soluble coffee in the book, more usually known as instant coffee in the UK. Powdered types of soluble coffee will mix more easily than granules, check the brand. Look out for espresso powder which has a good flavour and mixes easily.

STORECUPBOARD VOCABULARY

Terms may vary from the UK to the USA. I've made a list of instances where we might use different words for the same thing:

UK TERM – US TERM

plain flour – all purpose flour

baking tray, baking sheet – cookie sheet, sheet pan

bicarbonate of soda – baking soda

caster (or castor) sugar – superfine sugar

clingfilm – Saran wrap/plastic wrap

cornflour – cornstarch (the thickening agent, a white powder)

desiccated coconut – flaked coconut

double cream – heavy cream (48% butterfat)

glacé – candied

baking paper – baking parchment

ground almonds – almond flour

icing sugar – powdered, 10X, or confectioner's sugar

rosewater – some US brands labelled rosewater are in fact concentrated essence, please use just a few drops, and taste as you go

single cream – light cream

unsalted butter – don't assume butter labelled "sweet butter" is unsalted. It can be both, check the packaging.

whipping cream – light whipping cream (30–36% butterfat), heavy whipping (only one kind in UK) cream (36–40% butterfat). Choose light whipping cream where whipping cream is indicated in these recipes

whisk (verb) – beat, whip

full-fat (full-cream) milk – whole milk, regular milk, not skimmed or semi-skimmed milk. UK and US whole milk has the same butterfat content.

SOMETHING FOR TEATIME
Teacakes, tuiles, biscuits or even ice cream

At 4 o'clock, find a picturesque spot, eat a madeleine, and watch the world go by

When we've been spoiling ourselves (or just sheltering from the rain) sitting cosy in tea salons in the autumn and winter months, there are plenty of opportunities to enjoy our 4 o'clock *goûter* outdoors when the Parisian weather is more clement.

Many bijou jewels in the *pâtisserie* or *chocolaterie* crown are boutiques more reminiscent of a museum, where you leave with your preferred masterpiece, swinging a designer pastry bag over the wrist. Stroll on to a romantic leafy square with a fountain, a regal garden or sit under the shade of a cherry tree next to the River Seine to savour their exquisite masterpieces.

Several central large parks in Paris are ideally situated for picnic stops near sweet delectable addresses: notably the Luxembourg gardens, the Tuileries and les *Jardins des Plantes* (*La Ménagerie* has picnic tables where you can watch the exotic birds). You'll discover that there are also much smaller parks or squares in abundance, especially for these romantic springtime moments of sunshine, when the rain showers of March and April are often happily replaced by drizzling confetti of cherry and apple blossom petals and horse

chestnut trees brighten the squares with their flowering candles. In summer, enjoy the fragrant shade of lime blossom trees and don't forget that you can safely drink the water (*l'eau potable*) from the Wallace Fountains, which are scattered around the city.

I've included many of my favourite stopping off examples, as a sweet Parisian treasure hunt.

The following easy cake recipes are perfect to get started on our pâtisserie walk. They're traditionally made using classic moulds that require buttering or oiling beforehand but I prefer to use non-stick silicone moulds, simply because they're easier to use as they cut out that extra step – and the end result is just as good. If you haven't used a piping bag before, experiment with it by piping out the batter for madeleines and financiers and you'll see how easy it becomes!

Some of them are transportable treats, perfect for those moments when you need a quick sugar rush, resting on a park bench in between museum stops.

Honey, Rose and Green Tea Madeleines

MADELEINES AU MIEL, ROSE ET THÉ VERT

Nut free

Makes 18 classic or 48 mini cakes
Preparation time: 20 minutes

Resting time: 30 minutes (or 2 hours
    min, best overnight if you prefer the
    characteristic French bump)
Cooking time: 10 minutes
Temperature: 180°C/360°F fan (Gas 6)

2 tbsps milk
1 tbsp rosewater (see note on page 30)
1 tsp vanilla extract
100g butter, melted
1 ½ tbsps honey
60g caster sugar
2 eggs
120g flour
1 tsp baking powder
1 tsp matcha green tea powder

Serve shortly after baking with a cup
of light Darjeeling, green tea, or – as
in Proust's novel – dip it into a herbal
infusion like verbena and walk down
memory lane

This delicate scallop-shaped teacake (or *friand* for our Australian and New Zealand readers) not only has its own Square (**Place de la Madeleine** of course), but it's the address of the Parisian gourmet store Fauchon that has some of the best madeleines (and éclairs and macarons) in Paris.

How many times have we experienced *la Madeleine de Proust* when biting into something, and we suddenly – and involuntarily – remember an emotional moment from our childhood? My soggy egg and tomato sandwiches on a rained-out Scottish beach, with stewed tea in a flask, watching the view from the car, doesn't quite have the same sweet appeal as the French metaphor that arose from Marcel Proust's novel, *À la recherche du temps perdu (In Search of Lost Time)*; but it's a happy memory that provokes the most pleasurable goose-bumps around my taste-buds.

Madeleines are not originally from Paris; otherwise, with their traditional hump they could have been called Notre-Dames or Quasi-modos. So why Madeleines and not Hunchbacks? Instead they are a speciality of Commercy, where the name Madeleine stuck from the 18th century. The original Madeleine was said to have used rosewater, and, since there's *matcha do about* infusing tea into cakes in Paris these days, add a teaspoon of matcha green tea powder instead of the more classic lemon flavour. If you prefer your madeleines with the traditional hump in the middle, then prepare the mixture the day before and leave the batter to rest overnight in the fridge. Another tip for the perfect hunchback look is to chill your moulds first.

1   Heat together the milk with the rosewater, vanilla and honey.

2   Whisk the eggs and sugar in a bowl until light and frothy.

3   Melt the butter in the microwave or in a saucepan – or make a *beurre noisette* (see page 31).

4   Add the warm fragranced milk to the egg mix, then whisk in the flour, baking powder and melted (or browned) butter. Mix in the green tea powder.

5 Leave the mixture to rest in the fridge for 30 minutes. Otherwise, if you prefer the characteristic French hump, leave the mixture for at least 2 hours or covered in the fridge overnight (best option).

6 Chill the moulds in the fridge. Preheat the oven to 180°C/360°F fan (Gas 6). Transfer the mixture to a piping bag if filling for mini madeleines, or, using a spoon for the classic size, fill the mixture into cold silicone madeleine moulds about $^2/_3$–$^3/_4$ to the top. Place on a baking sheet and bake in the oven for 10 minutes (classic moulds) or 6–7 minutes (mini versions).

ROSEWATER

There are several recipes using rosewater in the book. I normally use light rosewater. This has the concentration of 3% rose essence to water. Take care which brand you buy – smaller bottles tend to contain a much more concentrated essence. If using an extract or essence, which is a concentrated flavouring, you will only need a few drops. And it is essential to add it slowly and taste as you go.

VARIATION

For lemon madeleines, replace rosewater with lemon juice and add the zest of an unwaxed lemon and omit the green tea. For chocolate madeleines, replace 20g flour with 100% unsweetened cocoa powder.

Beurre Noisette
BROWNED BUTTER

Preparation time: 10 minutes
Cooling time: 10 minutes

Unsalted butter

Browned butter is the magical yet simple detail that makes your little cakes full of flavour and adds that taste of Paris. Although it's traditionally used in *financier* cake recipes, I also love using this easy technique to add that *je ne sais quoi* to madeleines and crêpes, too.

1 Cut the amount of butter required in the recipe into small chunks. Gently melt in a saucepan over a medium heat until completely melted.

2 After about 5 minutes, or as soon as a foam starts to form, turn down the heat to low and leave for just another couple of minutes: that's all it takes for it to change colour so be careful not to burn it.

3 Filter out the grains using a sieve (although this is not essential: the taste is just as good).

4 Take off the heat and leave to cool slightly for about 10 minutes then continue with your recipe.

Almond Financier Teacakes

FINANCIERS

Makes approx. 18 classic financier cakes
  (or 30 mini financiers)
Preparation time: 15 minutes
Resting time: 10 minutes
Cooking time: 5 + 15 minutes
Temperature: 180°C/360°F fan (Gas 6)

140g egg whites (from approx. 4 eggs)
140g butter, cut roughly into bits
120g ground almonds (almond flour)
140g icing/confectioner's sugar
50g plain flour, sifted
Pinch salt
Few drops almond extract
Flaked almonds (optional, for decoration)

Serve with Darjeeling or jasmine green tea

VARIATIONS

Use **pistachios** instead
of the almonds; and
add any kind of **berries**,
dried apricot bits or
candied orange peel to
each cake before baking.

The *financier* almond teacake originated in Nancy (Lorraine) in the 17th Century as an oval shape, but it rose to Parisian fame in 1890 when a pastry chef (Monsieur Lasne) hit on a brilliant marketing idea and transformed it to a rectangular shape, resembling a gold bar, for his financial clientèle working at the stock exchange (*Place de la Bourse*) next door. Financiers are richer than their more cake-like cousins madeleines. Deliciously moist, nutty financier cakes are slightly crispy on the edges, and ridiculously rich in the best butter from Normandy, *Beurre d'Isigny*. Many pâtisseries and boulangeries take pride in using this for their more buttery specialities.

The financier's special taste comes from the *beurre noisette* (*noisette*: hazelnut): the butter is first melted in a saucepan until it browns slightly to create a wonderfully nutty flavour, as its French name suggests, see page 31. The financier batter can keep in the fridge for three days before baking. The cakes also freeze well for up to a month – great to have in stock for surprise teatimes with friends. Once baked, they are best eaten fresh on the day.

The oval shapes can still be found in many Parisian pâtisseries: likewise moulds can be found in Parisian bakery suppliers (see stockists); otherwise use the classic rectangular-shaped moulds.

1 Preheat the oven to 180°C/360°F fan (Gas 6). Measure out the egg white and set aside. Make "browned butter", page 31. Set aside to cool slightly for a few minutes.

2 Mix all the dry ingredients in a bowl. Add the egg whites and mix in the slightly cooled browned butter. Set aside to cool for about 10 minutes.

3 Using a spoon, fill silicone moulds (right to the top) and top each with flaked almonds, if using. I also love to add a raspberry on top.

4 Place on a baking sheet and bake in the oven for 13–15 minutes.

5 Leave to cool down slightly in their moulds for 2–3 minutes, then turn out the financiers onto a wire rack to air.

Mini Chocolate and Pear Hazelnut Financiers

FINANCIERS NOISETTE, CHOCOLAT ET POIRE

Gluten free

Makes 75 (enough for 3 trays of mini
  financier moulds, 25-cavity)
Preparation time: 15 minutes
Resting time: 10 minutes
Cooking time: 15 minutes
Temperature: 180°C/360°F fan (Gas 6)

140g egg whites (from approx. 4 eggs)
140g butter
120g ground hazelnuts
140g icing sugar
2 tbsps cocoa powder (100%
unsweetened)
40g chestnut flour, sifted (plain/
all-purpose flour can be substituted)
1 tsp salt
Half a pear, cut into bite sizes
Leftover hazelnut praline (optional,
recipe on page 171)

Serve with Assam or Oolong teas

MINI MOULDS

If you use mini moulds,
it's so much quicker to
pipe the mixture into the
moulds using a piping
bag.

Financiers are particularly rich in butter (but without it, or with much less, it's not a financier). Mini versions are popular in many pâtisseries such as Eric Kayser, sold in dainty little packages. Their little-but-decadent, rectangular, gold-nugget charm makes them difficult to resist and, just as they are delicious at teatime, they are also ideal served as *mignardises*, mini cakes served at the end of a meal with coffee.

Financiers are traditionally made with ground almonds, but you can substitute any nuts such as pistachios or, as in this recipe, enjoy chocolate and hazelnuts in every bite. If you have stored any leftover praline from page 171, then a sprinkle of that on top before baking intensifies the hazelnut flavours.

This version is also gluten free because of the **chestnut flour**. This can be found in health food shops or specialist *épiceries* (grocery stores). If you're not worried about gluten or if unable to find chestnut flour, for classic financiers replace the chestnut flour with the same amount of normal plain (all-purpose) flour.

1 Preheat the oven to 180°C/360°F fan (Gas 6). Measure out the egg whites and set aside. Make "browned butter", page 31. Set aside to cool slightly.

2 Meanwhile, weigh and mix all the dry ingredients in a bowl. Using a spoon or spatula, mix in the egg whites then add the browned butter.

3 Cool in the fridge for 10 minutes, to make it easier to spoon or pipe the batter in to the moulds.

4 Spoon (or pipe, with mini moulds I find it quicker) ¾ full into the silicone moulds (if you over fill them they do lose their gold nugget shape), placing a small piece of pear in the centre of each, and bake in the oven for about 10 minutes for mini moulds (and 13–15 minutes if you use larger classic-size moulds.)

5 Turn out the financiers onto a wire rack to cool. Best eaten fresh on the day of baking but you could store in an airtight container until the next day.

RUE
DE LA BANQUE

2ᵉ Arrᵗ

Mini Tigrés

IT'S NOT JUST THE KIDS WHO POUNCE ON THEM!

Makes approx. 18 mini tigrés, using mini savarin moulds/pans (18 cavity).
Preparation time: 15 minutes
Chilling time: 10 minutes
Cooking time: 10 + 10 minutes
Temperature: 180°C/360°F fan (Gas 6)

Batter:
70g egg whites (from approx. 2 eggs)
70g butter
60g ground almonds (almond flour)
70g icing sugar
25g plain flour, sifted
40g chocolate drops (or, if you prefer a fruity option, 20g fresh or frozen blueberries)
½ tsp vanilla extract
Pinch salt

Ganache:
50g dark chocolate, broken up into bits or grated
45g single cream

Serve with Assam or Oolong teas or a glass of milk

When my children first saw little *tigrés* sitting on the top of a pâtisserie counter, they instantly pounced on them. Tigrés ("tiger cakes", so-called because of the stripy chocolate effect on their surface) are little financier cakes baked in savarin moulds. They have little hollows, which are filled with a decadent centre of soft, dark chocolate *ganache*. Ganache is just a fancy term for melted chocolate and cream, often used as a cake filling or covering.

At first I thought they were difficult to make but you just need mini savarin silicone moulds. *Bonjour*, tiger! Thereafter the hardest part is self-control: resist the temptation of devouring the whole lot before *les enfants* leap on them. Well they are mini, after all.

Adding *beurre noisette* (page 31), browned butter, gives the tigrés that extra nutty flavour but, if you want to save time, you can simply add melted butter and skip step 2. Tigrés are best eaten on the same day as they are baked but they freeze well, if you have any leftovers.

1 Preheat the oven to 180°C/360°F fan (Gas 6). Measure out the egg whites and set aside. Make "browned butter", page 31. Set aside to cool slightly.

2 Mix all the dry ingredients (except the chocolate drops or blueberries) in a bowl and gradually mix in the egg whites, vanilla and the browned butter. Mix in the chocolate drops (or blueberries).

3 Chill in the fridge for about 10 minutes. This will make it easier to spoon or pipe out the mixture.

4 Spoon or pipe into the mini silicone moulds (right to the top). Bake in the oven for 8–10 minutes or until golden brown.

5 Make the ganache. Heat the cream in a small saucepan to nearly boiling, then pour half of the hot cream over the chocolate. Stir with a wooden spoon until the chocolate starts to melt then add the rest of the hot cream and stir until the ganache is beautifully smooth. Set aside to cool.

6 When the tigrés have cooled down slightly in their moulds turn them out onto a wire rack.

7 Using a spatula, fill a piping bag with the ganache and, using a plain tip, pipe out little heaps into the tigré hollows.

CHOCOLATE DROPS

Instead of making a chocolate ganache, gently press a few chocolate drops or bits of broken chocolate directly into the hollows as soon as you have turned the hot cakes out of their moulds onto a wire tray.

VARIATION

Omit the chocolate and add 20g fresh or frozen blueberries to the batter mix. Fill each cavity with a blueberry (ideally with a fresh one but frozen will do) in place of the chocolate ganache.

Alternatively, pipe a fruity pastry cream, such as the one on page 140, into the hollows.

Diamond Biscuits

DIAMANTS

Makes approx. 20 biscuits
Prep time: 15 minutes
Chilling time: 25 minutes
Cooking time: 8 minutes
Temperature: 180°C/360°F fan (Gas 6)

125g butter, softened
45g sugar (granulated, if possible)
½ tsp vanilla extract
150g plain flour

Serve with Lady Grey tea or Darjeeling, the Champagne of teas

My daughter, Lucie, loves swooning over the glistening window displays of high-end jewellers in **Place Vendôme**. She also adores making these biscuits, as they are addictively soft and crumbly for something so simple. What's more, if you've run out of eggs it's a perfect recipe to have up your sleeve.

Diamants are the French equivalent of shortbread and, when rolled in granulated sugar, they glisten like diamonds. You could say that Lucie's in the sky with these diamants!

If you're in Place Vendôme and feel like splashing out for a special occasion, then pop in for afternoon tea at the Ritz or any of the other grand hotels nearby such as the Mandarin Oriental, the Meurice, or the Crillon, for example, and make an afternoon of it.

1 Mix the butter and sugar until light and creamy, either using a balloon whisk or in a stand mixer using the flat (or paddle) beater. Add the vanilla extract and gradually add the flour. Keep mixing until the batter forms into a ball. (At this stage you could add a different flavour such as cinnamon.)

2 Roll the dough out onto a floured surface, ensuring you roll it as round as possible into a sausage, to about 3cm (1¼") in diameter. Roll in cling film and chill in the fridge for 25 minutes. Meanwhile, preheat the oven to 180°C/360°F fan (Gas 6).

3 Once chilled, roll in the sugar then cut into 1cm-thick (approx. ⅜") discs. Place them on a baking sheet lined with baking paper or a silicone mat and bake for 8 minutes until golden.

SHAPING

To keep your sausage shape round in the fridge, without a flat side, roll in cling film and place it on top of a plate covered in rice.

Coconut Macaroons

ROCHERS COCO

Gluten and nut free

Makes approx. 10
Preparation: 10 minutes
Cooking time: 10–12 minutes
Chilling time: 20 minutes
Temperature: 180°C/360°F fan (Gas 6)

90g sugar
1 tbsp honey
125g desiccated/shredded coconut
75g egg whites (from approx. 2 eggs)
70g dark cooking chocolate (64%)

Serve with jasmine green tea, a spicy chai,
or hot chocolate

I could be richer than butter by now if I had earned a euro or two for everyone who asked me "Do you call them maca*roons* or maca-*rons?*"

They are, of course, referring to the Parisian macaron (more on that in the chapter on page 143–177). This is a macaroon. It still uses egg whites but, instead of ground almonds, these simpler treats are made with coconut. You can coat the bottoms in chocolate but they are just as good and quicker to make without.

1   Preheat the oven to 180°C/360°F fan (Gas 6).

2   Stir the honey and sugar in a bain-marie (a double boiler, i.e. a glass bowl over a pot of simmering water) until the sugar has melted.

3   Take off the heat and add the coconut and egg whites. Mix well for a couple of minutes. Moisten your hands with some water and form the coconut mix into little balls.

4   Place them on a baking tray covered with either baking paper or a silicone mat, and press them down to form little heaps.

5   Bake for 10–12 minutes then place on a wire rack to cool.

6   Melt the chocolate in a bain-marie. When the macaroons are cool, dip the bottoms in the melted chocolate. Return to the baking tray and chill in the fridge until set for about 20 minutes.

7   Best eaten fresh but can be stored in an airtight container until next day.

Hot Chocolate

CHOCOLAT CHAUD

Gluten and nut free

Enough for 2 rich servings

240g full-cream milk
90g dark chocolate (70%)
Good pinch nutmeg or gingerbread spice
(*pain d'épices*)
Pinch of sea salt (or *fleur de sel*)

Serve with almond tuiles

If you're a chocoholic, then take the plunge into chocolate euphoria by tasting Paris's designer chocolatiers' offerings – ranging from plain, fruity, praline and spicy flavours to adventurous chocolate combinations that are truly out of the box. Some chocolatiers have a *salon de thé* or even a "chocolate bar". Jean-Paul Hévin in **Rue Saint Honoré** and some – like Angelina's in **Rue de Rivoli** – serve chocolate as velvety as their seating upholstery. One of my favourite tea salons, Un Dimanche à Paris, with a chocolate theme – in **Saint Germain's Cour du Commerce Saint-André** – serves their memorable *chocolat chaud* in a typical porcelain chocolate pot with a plunger (*moussoir*), à la Marie-Antoinette.

A spoon-clingingly intense chocolat chaud from a Parisian tea salon is more than just a mug of cocoa. Chocolate boutiques use good quality dark chocolate: the higher the cocoa content, the less sweet and more naturally intense the flavour is.

1 Heat the milk. Add the spice, salt and broken chocolate, stirring with a wooden spoon until melted and smooth. Be careful not to boil.

2 Froth up using a hand mixer or, even simpler, use a milk frother (I have a battery-operated hand one which cost me very little and does the job best!).

3 Depending on the chocolate's bitterness, you could add some sugar to taste but it doesn't really need it, letting the earthiness of the chocolate shine through.

SPICES

If you like a touch of spice, infuse a cinnamon stick, add some finely grated ginger, a pinch of chilli or *piment d'espelette*. Alternatively add orange peel, or a simple touch of vanilla to your love potion, just like the Parisian chocolatiers do.

Almond Tuiles

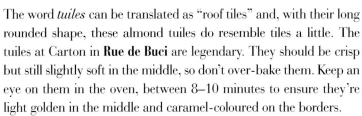

TUILES AUX AMANDES

Makes approx. 15
Preparation time: 10 minutes
Chilling time: 10 minutes
Cooking time: 10 minutes
Temperature: 170°C/340°F fan (Gas 3)

75g egg whites (from approx. 2 eggs)
75g caster sugar (superfine sugar)
35g plain flour
75g butter, melted
1 tsp grated unwaxed orange peel
(optional)
75g flaked almonds

Served with hot chocolate, speciality tea
or ice cream

The word *tuiles* can be translated as "roof tiles" and, with their long rounded shape, these almond tuiles do resemble tiles a little. The tuiles at Carton in **Rue de Buci** are legendary. They should be crisp but still slightly soft in the middle, so don't over-bake them. Keep an eye on them in the oven, between 8–10 minutes to ensure they're light golden in the middle and caramel-coloured on the borders.

The customary rounded shape can be achieved by pressing them over a rolling pin (or in a sieve) but I've found it much easier and quicker to simply nestle the ends into the grooves of the pastry rack; they shape instantly as they cool. Alternatively, they do taste just as good flat!

1 Preheat the oven to 170°C/340°F fan (Gas 3). Mix all the ingredients together in a bowl. Leave the batter to cool in the fridge for 10 minutes (to make it easier to spoon out).

2 Line two baking sheets with baking paper or a silicone mat and spoon out the mixture into oval discs – using the back of the spoon – to about 6cm (2½") in diameter.

3 Bake in the oven for 8–10 minutes or until golden in the middle and brown on the edges. Bake in two batches (in order to be able to shape them while still hot).

4 Straight from the oven (hold delicately as they're hot but easy to bend at this stage), tease one end into the grooves of a pastry rack and slightly bend the tuile to nestle the other end to shape them into the traditional tuiles shape as they cool.

5 Tuiles can keep another day if stored in an airtight container, so you can make the pleasure last even longer.

Canelés

CANELÉS DE BORDEAUX

Nut free

Makes approx. 16
Preparation time: 20 minutes
Resting time (for batter): 8–12 hours (or overnight. This is for best results but it can be less)
Cooking time: 50 minutes
Temperature: 180°C/360°F fan (Gas 4) for a silicone mould

2 vanilla pods (or 4 tsps good vanilla extract)
500ml whole milk
120g flour
200g sugar
2 eggs
2 egg yolks
50g butter
3 tbsps dark rum

Serve slightly warm from the oven with a Ceylon or Keemun tea

Although these pretty-shaped cakes are in most Parisian pâtisseries, they are a speciality of Bordeaux. Because egg whites were used to clarify Bordeaux wines, the local nuns saved the yolks and with them invented *canelas* in the 18th century. Over the years these treats took on various different looks and names.

It's funny to see that even the French are sometimes confused about how to spell this: either **cannelé** or **canelé**. Apparently, as of 1985, one "n" was officially dropped and now its true identity is found in the shop especially dedicated to this aromatic teatime treat in **Rue Saint-Dominique**, at Lemoine.

What makes the canelé so delicious is its dark, caramelised crispy outside while the soft interior is bright, eggy yellow, airy and spongy. Traditionally fragranced with vanilla, it's also French-kissed with rum. It took me a while to realise that they really do need to spend all that time in the oven. I was scared that they were burning but the darker they are, the better. If they're undercooked they become hopelessly mushy inside and can shrivel like a forgotten accordion. I strongly recommend using two vanilla pods but, if you don't have any, replace them with four teaspoons of good vanilla extract.

The traditional way to make canelés is with copper moulds. French chefs stipulate greasing them with beeswax but it's easier to spray them with culinary non-stick oil. As a lazy gourmet, I use silicone moulds. They are perhaps not quite as "pro" as the classic copper, but silicone moulds are easier to find, they're so much easier to wash and the final product tastes just as good!

If you do use copper moulds, then bake at 240°C/500°F fan (Gas 9) for 10 minutes, then turn down the oven to 180°C/360°F fan (Gas 4) and bake for a further 40 minutes. I've adjusted the oven temperature accordingly in this recipe using silicone moulds, as they don't like high temperatures.

Canelés de Bordeaux are best eaten fresh on the day so if you don't use all the batter, keep it another couple of days in the fridge and use just the amount you need. The batter can also be frozen for up to two weeks – just decant it into a jam jar.

1 Split the vanilla pods lengthways down the middle using a sharp knife and scrape out the seeds. Add the vanilla seeds and pod to the milk in a saucepan and, as soon as it comes to the boil, take off the heat, cover and leave the vanilla to infuse for at least 20 minutes.

2 Sift and mix together the flour and sugar. Add the eggs and yolks all in one go and hand-whisk briskly until there are no lumps but a smooth, thick paste.

3 Remove the vanilla pod from the milk and gently reheat (but don't boil).

4 Cut up the butter roughly and melt into the hot vanilla milk.

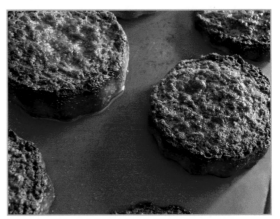

5 Gradually whisk the hot milk into the egg mix, so there are no lumps. The batter will be smooth and runny, almost like a batter for crêpes.

6 Add the rum then leave the fragrant mix to rest in the fridge for 8–12 hours or overnight.

7 When ready to bake, preheat the oven to 180°C/ 360°F fan (Gas 4).

8 Hand-whisk the chilled batter well for a minute and, using a pouring jug, fill the moulds nearly to the top. Place on a rimmed baking sheet and bake for about 50 minutes to an hour, depending on whether you like them dark gold or dark – almost black. Don't be afraid to see them going pretty brown at the top after 40 minutes; leave them in for another 10–15 minutes, as you'll discover that they'll still be spongy and light on the inside.

9 Turn the canelés out of the moulds straight away and leave to cool on a wire rack.

RUE
SAINT-DOMINIQUE

7ᵉ Arrᵗ

Orange Crêpes
SUZETTE STYLE

Nut free

Makes approx. 12
Preparation time: 10 minutes
Resting time: 30 minutes (optional)
Cooking time: 30 minutes (or half the
time if you have 2 crêpe pans!)

40g butter, melted (or browned butter —
beurre noisette, page 31)
250g plain (all-purpose) flour (or half
and half plain and wholemeal)
½ tsp salt
2 tbsps icing sugar
3 eggs
500g semi-skimmed milk
1 tbsp Grand Marnier™ (or orange
blossom water)
2 tsps finely grated unwaxed orange zest

Serve with Normandy cider (doux), iced
tea or Ceylon tea with milk

Some of the best crêpes are found at the Breizh café on **Rue Vieille du Temple** but if you don't feel like sitting in a tearoom, brasserie or café, then there's usually someone selling crêpes on some Parisian street corner. While you sit by the nearest fountain and watch the world go by, a thin crêpe spread with any of the classics like chocolate or *confiture* (jam) is a perfect pick-me-up. When we serve them at home, the basic sugar-and-squeeze-of-lemon remains a favourite, as is express fruit jam. The toughest decision is whether to roll or fold them!

The French not only celebrate *Mardi Gras* (Shrove Tuesday) with these wafer-thin pancakes but they also traditionally flip them during *La Chandeleur* (Candlemass), which marks the halfway point between the shortest day and the spring equinox in February. Tradition goes that if you manage to catch the pancake by holding a coin in your writing hand whilst flipping the pancake with the other, your family will be prosperous for the rest of the year — although the French flip pancakes at any time of year and enjoy them at breakfast, lunch, goûter or dinner!

The addition of orange and *beurre noisette* (page 31) is my express teatime take on the *crêpes Suzette* dessert. If you do have time to let the batter rest for at least 30 minutes, the crêpes will be lighter. If you can find *farine fluide* ("type 45" thinner flour), then there is no need to sift the flour.

1 Prepare browned butter, page 31, or use melted butter.

2 Sift the flour and icing sugar into a large bowl and add the salt. Make a well in the middle and break the eggs into it.

3 Add about a quarter of the milk and, using a hand whisk, beat the mixture well until you have a smooth, thick paste. Gradually add the rest of the milk and the Grand Marnier™.

4 Add the browned (or melted) butter and orange zest. Leave to rest for about half an hour at room temperature (this is for the gluten to expand in the mix, making the batter lighter, although it's not essential in this recipe). The mix will look quite runny but this is perfectly normal.

5 Ladle one small quantity of the batter into a very hot crêpe pan that has been brushed with butter (or wiped with butter on kitchen paper). Swirl the batter round the pan quickly, as thinly as you can, covering the surface of the pan. Cook over a medium-high heat for about 2–3 minutes until bubbles form on the surface. Using a spatula or your fingertips, quickly flip the crêpe over and cook for another couple of minutes.

6 Turn down the heat slightly (but still at medium) and repeat the process, topping up with a brushing of butter in the pan, until you have about 12 crêpes (depending on pan size), stacking them aside on a large plate.

TEMPERATURE

Keep the crêpes warm by stacking them on a plate and cover with an inverted plate on top. The first crêpe is notoriously known for not being good? Not so! Just keep the pan extra hot for the first one, then turn the heat down to medium-high for the rest.

VARIATION

For chocolate and orange crêpes, add 1 tbsp unsweetened cocoa powder to the flour in step 1.

Speculoos Ice Cream

GLACE "SPECULOOS"

Preparation time: 15 minutes
Cooking time: 15 minutes
Chilling time: 2 hours (or overnight)
Freezing time: 2–3 hours

500g (½ litre) full-cream milk
1 vanilla pod / bean
100g light brown sugar
6 egg yolks
100g speculoos spread / Biscoff Spread /
cookie butter
4 speculoos biscuits (optional)

Serve with almond tuiles or more
speculoos biscuits

It's not just Belgian chocolate that has wooed Paris over the years. Their famous spicy, brown-sugared cinnamon biscuits, called *Speculoos*, are now a particularly Parisian treat too. Speculoos have an addictive cinnamon flavour and an intriguing salty taste. Ever since my children saw that their favourite biscuit now exists as a spread (easily available online and called *Biscoff Spread* in the UK), they love to paste it on crêpes, waffles and on a plain, fresh crusty baguette. Put this in ice cream and I have the girls melting quicker than the ice cream!

If you're looking for ice cream in Paris, most Parisians point you in the direction of Berthillon on **Ile-Saint-Louis**. It's no shock that the queues there are particularly impressive in the summer months but the main surprise is in August. As the majority of Parisians close their doors for a month during the annual summer holidays, so does this ice cream institution. Who said the ice cream business was only seasonal? Don't worry, many vendors sell their ice cream throughout Paris, so find a spot next to the **Seine**, refresh yourself with lip-smacking seasonal flavours and watch the *Bâteaux-Mouches* fly past.

If you're also mad about macarons, you'll love to find an excuse to use up plenty of leftover egg yolks. Ice cream – real, custardy ice cream – is one of my favourite egg-yolk recipes, as it can use up to six yolks in this easy, classic recipe. There's no need to worry if you don't have an ice-cream maker; this rich ice cream is also easily made by hand.

1 Chill a bowl in the fridge for step 5.

2 Split the vanilla pod lengthways down the middle using a sharp knife and scrape out the seeds. In a medium saucepan, heat the milk over a medium heat.

3 In a separate bowl, whisk together the sugar, yolks and speculoos paste until pale and creamy.

4 When the milk begins to boil, pour some of the hot milk over the yolk mix and whisk. Gradually whisk in the rest of the milk then return to the pan

over a low to medium heat, whisking constantly until the cream thickens. Be careful not to boil the mixture at this stage or you'll overcook the eggs and risk curdling them. It's ready as soon as the mixture can coat/cling to a spoon (see picture below).

5   Pour the mixture into the chilled bowl and refrigerate for at least 2 hours (I often leave it overnight).

6   Transfer to an ice cream maker (I use a stand mixer with ice cream attachment and churn until it starts to harden after about 20 minutes). Follow the ice cream maker's instructions.

7   Meanwhile, crush the speculoos biscuits (if using) and, just before the end of churning the ice cream, add the broken biscuits to the mix and turn a couple of minutes more, just to incorporate the biscuits.

8   Transfer to an ice cream carton and freeze for at least 2–3 hours.

MAKING ICE CREAM WITHOUT A MACHINE

If you don't have an ice-cream maker, transfer the cold custard mix to a large, durable tin and freeze for up to an hour.

Take out of the freezer and, using a spatula, beat in the iced-up border particles until it's back to a smooth mix. Return to the freezer and repeat this operation every 30 minutes for a couple of hours (this also works for the Rose Ice Cream recipe, page 60).

Mix in the crushed speculoos biscuits in the last mixing, when you see it's looking more like ice-cream.

SEPARATING EGG YOLKS

Don't throw out your empties! This is a quick and nifty little trick that would have had me paying attention in science at school. Break your egg(s) onto a plate. Using a scrupulously clean plastic water bottle, squeeze it well in the middle and vacuum up the yolk(s) into the bottle, leaving the egg whites on the plate. Egg-citing! I would suggest at first (before you have this method cracked), practising with one egg at a time so that if you have any punctured yolks, any previous whites are not affected.

Eggs are easier to separate if you do so while they are still chilled.

The traditional method is to break the shells in the middle over a bowl, letting the whites fall and use the two half shells as cups to transfer the yolk from one to the other until all the white has fallen into the bowl.

Remember that egg yolks have to be consumed quickly (up to two days sealed in the fridge) but egg whites can keep for up to a week in a sealed jar in the fridge, and can be frozen.

For making macarons, leave egg whites ideally to rest for 3–5 days, no more. The older the egg white, the thinner it becomes and the meringue is weak. If you don't have time to make macarons after keeping it for 5 days, either freeze it or make financiers, tuiles or coconut macaroons.

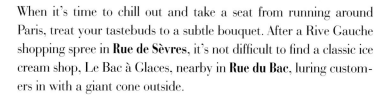

Rose Ice Cream

GLACE À LA ROSE

Gluten and nut free

Preparation time: 15 minutes
Cooking time: 15 minutes
Chilling time: 2 hours (or overnight)
Freezing time: 2–3 hours

300g full-cream milk
200g whipping cream
25ml rosewater (see page 30)
A few drops of pink food colouring
(optional)
100g caster sugar (superfine sugar)
1 tbsp dried milk powder
6 egg yolks

Fabulous served with fresh raspberries, an
almond tuile or a rose macaron

When it's time to chill out and take a seat from running around
Paris, treat your tastebuds to a subtle bouquet. After a Rive Gauche
shopping spree in **Rue de Sèvres**, it's not difficult to find a classic ice
cream shop, Le Bac à Glaces, nearby in **Rue du Bac**, luring customers in with a giant cone outside.

1 Chill a bowl in the fridge for step 5.

2 In a medium saucepan, heat together the milk and cream with the
   rosewater and pink colouring (if using).

3 In a separate bowl, whisk together the sugar, dried milk powder and yolks
   until pale and creamy.

4 Pour the warmed cream over the egg mix and return to the pan over a
   medium heat, whisking constantly until the cream thickens. It's ready
   when it can coat a spoon.

5 Pour the mixture into the chilled bowl and refrigerate for at least a couple
   of hours.

6 Transfer to an ice cream maker and churn until ready. Spoon into an ice
   cream carton and freeze for a couple of hours. See page 58 for instructions
   on making without an ice cream maker.

CHOUX TIME!
Éclairs and Cream Puffs

What choux size are you: chouquette, cream puff, éclair or religieuse?

Choux dough is genius. It's not only the basis for French classics such as éclairs, choux puffs, profiteroles, *religieuses* and the Saint-Honoré, but the best part is that it's straightforward and relatively quick to make.

What started out as *pâte à chaud*, meaning hot dough, since it was dried out by heating directly in the pan or casserole, has somehow, along the years – as if playing "Chinese whispers" – developed into *pâte à choux*. Some say the French thought it looked like little cabbages (chou), but then they also think a religieuse pastry (a double-decker choux bun) looks like a nun. I'm sticking with the pâte à chaud story.

Made only with water/milk, butter, flour and eggs, the humidity of the dough magically puffs it up in the oven without using any yeast or raising agents.

When perfectly cooked, choux is slightly crispy on the outside and the inside is beautifully light, airy and soft (but cooked through, not mushy). The golden rule is to ensure they're baked enough before taking them out of the oven.

If undercooked, they'll collapse. So here's a word in your ear: follow the tips and instructions to the letter and you'll be hooked on all different choux sizes.

As the dough can last for up to three days in the fridge, it's a great idea to make a good quantity of it and use the rest for clever "leftovers". If you only use some of it, keep it (still in the piping bag) in the fridge, remove 20 minutes before you need to bake (to bring up to room temperature) and in very little time you can produce *chouquettes*, choux buns, éclairs, and religieuses. If you have a waffle pan, conjure up light, round choux waffles in no time – there's no need to use yeast! To make profiteroles for dessert, fill choux puffs with ice cream and dribble on chocolate sauce.

If you haven't used a piping bag before, then I suggest you start with chouquettes, then puffs or waffles, move on to éclairs, then finish off with a towering *religieuse*.

The éclairs and pastel-shaded choux puffs of the boutiques of Paris, with their light, fragranced fillings, have been my inspiration. Mentioned throughout the text are some of my favourite pâtisserie spots.

Choux Pastry

ÉCLAIR OR CREAM PUFF PASTRY

Nut free

Makes approx. 50 choux puffs; 16 éclairs
  (makes 660g dough)
Preparation time: 15 minutes
Cooking time: 15–30 minutes
Temperature: 160°C/320°F fan (Gas 4)

150g water
100g milk
1 tsp sea salt (or *fleur de sel*)
2 tbsps sugar
90g butter (cut into small cubes)
150g flour (plain, all-purpose)
4 eggs (or 3 larger eggs), chilled

Serve with pastry cream (page 72) or
crème légère (page 74)

Choux dough can also be made without the milk: instead just use 250g water. This is a large quantity but as it keeps in the fridge for up to four days, I find it handy to have the dough still in its piping bag, ready for a quick something-I-rustled-up-earlier treat. Otherwise just halve the quantity. This recipe may look long but I'm taking your hand here so that you can have this mastered in no time!

1 Preheat the oven to 160°C/320°F fan (Gas 4). Boil the water, milk, salt, sugar and butter (cut roughly into bits/cubes) in a large saucepan. Cut the butter up into pieces: if you put in big slabs, by the time it has melted the liquid will have evaporated too much.

2 Once boiling, remove from the heat and quickly add the flour. Mix well for a couple of minutes with a wooden spoon or spatula (or sturdy balloon whisk) until the dough is smooth and naturally comes away from the sides of the pan.

3 Transfer the dough to a mixing bowl and leave to cool for about 5 minutes. Gradually add the eggs, incorporating them well, one by one (I mix by hand using a wooden spoon or rubber spatula but it's just as quick using an electric stand mixer with a flat beater). After each addition, the dough will break up (see photo, top left) and look rather sloppy. Don't worry. Keep mixing well, incorporating air into the dough until you have a smooth, thick paste.

4 Transfer the dough to a piping bag fitted with a tip (depending on the recipe, but usually a 12mm (½") tip is great). At this point you can pipe out straight away or keep the dough refrigerated in the bag for up to four days.

5 Pipe out small heaps (according to the recipe) on baking trays covered in baking paper/parchment or a silicone mat. Push down the dough, now and again, using the pastry scraper. Leave a 5cm (2") between each mound, as they will spread out during baking. They do have a funny shape when you pipe them, but in the oven you'll see them even out and puff up into little balls. If they have pointed tops, tap them down lightly with your fingertips.

6 Bake in the oven for 15–30 minutes, according to the recipe. **Don't open the oven door during baking**, as they might collapse! Wait until they are cooked enough and have turned from golden to mid-brown, then they are ready to remove from the oven. Leave to cool well before garnishing (you can even keep them until the next day).

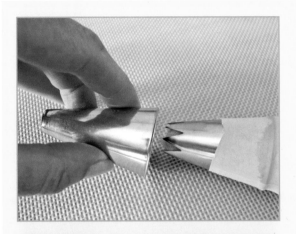

FOR PERFECT CHOUX

To pipe éclairs, I like using a 12mm (½") serrated tip, although a plain tip will give you just as good results. For standard éclairs pipe out strips of about 12cm (4¾") long, as they will puff out during cooking.

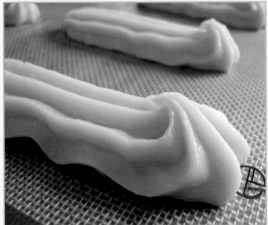

If you have choux pastry in a piping bag already with a serrated tip and later want to change to a plain tip, then there's no need to change piping bags: simply pop another tip on top and pipe away. (See photo, top left.)

Ensure the choux pastry is cooked enough. If they're slightly undercooked, they risk flattening when you take them out of the oven.

3e Arrt

RUE
DU
PONT AUX CHOUX

Shiny Choux Glaze
GLAÇAGE

Quick glaze:
Preparation time: 10 minutes
Cooking time: 5 minutes
Cooling time: 20 minutes

2g gelatine (1 x 2g sheet)
80g single cream
20g water
20g honey
120g white chocolate, broken into bits
A pinch of colouring (optional, according to recipe)

Chocolate glaze:
Preparation time: 10 minutes
Cooking time: 10 minutes
Chilling time: 2 hours

4g gelatine (2 x 2g sheets)
100g sugar
30g cocoa powder (100% unsweetened)
30g water
70g single cream

Peek into many chic Parisian pâtisseries and you'll see éclairs or puffs proudly parade a simple powdering of icing sugar, with fruity decorations doing the dressing up. However, an éclair isn't an éclair without a shiny, sticky glaze, especially for chocolate, coffee or caramel éclairs.

I'm lazy at making fondant glazes from scratch, wishing to avoid sugar thermometers over double boilers as much as you would perhaps wish to avoid long queues at the Eiffel Tower. Luckily, ready-made professional pouring fondant mix is becoming easier to find these days in speciality baking stores and supermarkets, (not to be confused with roll-on fondant icing for decorating cakes) but at the time of writing, it's still not universally easy to find the same kind of product everywhere. If you do find it, just follow the manufacturer's instructions. Otherwise, here's an alternative using cupboard ingredients so you can join the fast lane to glazing teatime éclairs.

The chocolate glaze below is also worth taking the time to chill in advance. However, if you are pushed for time to make a milk chocolate glaze, follow the Quick glaze recipe, replacing the 120g white chocolate with 110g milk chocolate.

QUICK GLAZE

1 Soak the gelatine in cold water for 10 minutes.

2 Heat the cream, water and honey (plus colouring, if using) in a saucepan until boiling, then take off the heat.

3 Squeeze the gelatine of excess water, and add to the hot cream. Mix briskly with a hand whisk until melted.

4 Add the white chocolate and mix until melted.

5 When smooth, set aside to cool for 15–20 minutes, then dip your choux puffs or éclairs into the glaze or spread it on.

CHOCOLATE GLAZE

1 Soak the gelatine in cold water for 10 minutes.

2 Boil the sugar with the cocoa powder and water, stirring occasionally. Take off the heat.

3 Boil the cream in another saucepan then add to the cocoa syrup. Whisk in the gelatine – which has been squeezed of any excess water – until smooth.

4 When cool, place in the fridge for at least 2 hours (or overnight) until needed.

5 When ready to use, reheat gently for 2 minutes then whisk well so that it is smooth. Dip your éclairs into the glaze, wiping off any excess with your finger.

6 Both glazes can keep in the fridge for up to a week in a sealed container and can also be frozen.

Choux Crumble Topping

CRAQUELIN

Preparation time: 10 minutes
Chilling time: 20 minutes
Cooking time: 15 minutes
Temperature: 160°C/320°F fan (Gas 4)

50g salted butter, softened
60g flour (plain, all-purpose)
60g light brown sugar

Why not add pumpkin spice, or gingerbread spice (*pain d'epices*) to your crumble mix

What's the latest craze on the Parisian choux puff catwalk?

When I first saw some particularly posh éclairs displayed in their shiny glass case, they had crinkly, crackly tops on them and were topped off with a dusting of icing sugar. They didn't have sticky fondant on them, just this sophisticated crumbly coating called *craquelin*. For something that looked a bit "rough" they were positively – and intriguingly – exquisite.

It sounds fancy but this éclair fashion frill is just a simple crumble mix of butter, flour and brown sugar, rolled out to a thin film, chilled then cut to size with either a cookie cutter or into strips and placed on choux buns or éclairs before baking.

Placing a little sheet of crumble topping before baking also helps ensure that your choux puffs puff up evenly. What's more, the sheets of crumble topping freeze well so it's handy to have a stock of them on call for quicker wow-factor moments.

1 Cream the softened butter. You could use a stand mixer but this is just as easy by hand with a wooden spoon.

2 Gradually mix in the brown sugar and flour. As soon as the mix is a smooth paste (it shouldn't look like breadcrumbs), transfer the ball of paste to a baking tray covered in baking paper/parchment.

3 Place another sheet of baking paper on top. Using a rolling pin, flatten out the crumble to about 3mm (⅛") thickness (too thin will make it difficult to handle later).

4 Transfer the sheet to the fridge and chill for about 20 minutes. Using a cookie cutter, press out circles of about 4cm (1¾") diameter (for choux buns of 4cm) then set aside to chill (or freeze) until needed.

5 Top the crumble discs on top of the choux puffs just before popping them in the oven.

Pastry Cream
CRÈME PÂTISSIÈRE

Gluten and nut free
(without the variations)

Preparation time: 10 minutes
Cooking time: 10 minutes
Chilling time: 1–2 hours

500g full-cream milk
1 Madagascan vanilla pod/bean (or 1 tsp extract)
6 egg yolks (see tip page 59)
80g caster sugar (superfine sugar)
40g cornflour (cornstarch)

Use it to fill macarons, millefeuilles, tarts and choux puffs

This straightforward classic custard cream is what gives your fruity tarts, choux puffs, éclairs and millefeuilles the *ooh-la-la* factor. Perfectly chilled, it's far removed from my hot-dolloped packet version in the *banana surprise* (page 12)! If your pastry cream is made using a good quality, sticky fat vanilla pod (or bean) then there's nothing "plain" about vanilla cream!

Pack a powerful vanilla punch with intense Madagascan Bourbon vanilla or, if you prefer a more subtle flavour, opt for Tahitian vanilla. It's best with a vanilla pod but if you can't find it, replace one pod with a teaspoon of vanilla extract. Many pastry chefs also whip in unsalted butter but I personally find it just as tasty without.

To personalise your pastries and adapt the flavours to citrus or summer fruits, chocolate, praline or coffee desserts, follow the simple variation guide (page 74). Pastry cream can keep in the fridge for up to two days.

1 Cut down the middle of the vanilla pod/bean lengthways with a sharp knife from top to bottom. Scrape out the seeds from each half and add to a saucepan with the milk. Gradually bring to the boil over a low-medium heat.

2 Meanwhile, in a mixing bowl, hand-whisk the yolks with the sugar until pale then whisk in the cornflour (cornstarch) until pale, smooth and creamy.

3 As soon as the milk starts to boil, pour half of the hot milk onto the yolk mix, whisk again and transfer back to the saucepan. Whisk continuously over a medium heat until thickened. Take off the heat as soon as you have the first couple of thick bubbles.

4 Place cling film (plastic wrap) directly in contact with the hot pastry cream, to avoid a film forming on top (you don't want to whisk this in later, otherwise you'll end up with a lumpy, bumpy cream!). Set aside and leave to cool before chilling in the fridge for at least an hour.

5 Once cool, remove the film and whisk the cream again to ensure it's beautifully smooth. At this stage you may need to add a little extra cream, depending on your chosen pastry (see light pastry cream on page 74).

6 Transfer the cream to a piping bag with a plain (or serrated, if you want it to look fancy) tip and pipe into choux puffs, éclairs or millefeuilles, or simply spoon in to your preferred tart.

Instead of the vanilla pod:

Citrus (Agrumes): Add the zest of an unwaxed lemon, orange or lime and sieve at the end of step one.

Chocolate (Chocolat): Add 100g dark chocolate at the end of cooking and whisk in while still warm; also ideal with warm spices such as ginger.

Coffee (Café): Add 2 tsps of soluble/instant coffee to the hot milk.

Elderflower/Rose/Violet (Fleur de Sureau/Rose/Violette): Reduce sugar by 20g and add 2 tbsps floral syrup after cooking. Good for strawberry/raspberry/blackberry desserts.

Hazelnut (Noisette): Add 80g of praline at the end of cooking (see Paris-Brest macaron recipe, page 171, up to step 6).

Pistachio (Pistache): Whisk 25g of pistachio paste (page 98) to the warming milk in step 1.

Crème Suzette: Add the zest of an unwaxed orange and sieve at the end of step 1. Add another 10g cornflour in step 2. At the end of cooking, whisk in 50g Grand Marnier™.

Tea or Herbal Infusions (Infusions de Thé): Infuse a tea bag into the hot milk then remove before continuing with step 2. Floral teas such as Earl Grey, Jasmine, and Verbena work particularly well.

Light Pastry Cream
CRÈME LÉGÈRE

250g pastry cream (chilled)
200g whipping cream
2 x 2g sheets of gelatine

1   Soak the gelatine in cold water for 15 minutes.

2   Measure out the whipping cream in a bowl and keep chilled.

3   Whisk the pastry cream until smooth. Take out a couple of spoonfuls of the pastry cream and heat in a small bowl for 25 seconds in the microwave.

4   Add the gelatine and stir until dissolved into the cream.

5   Whip the whipping cream until quite stiff then fold in the rest of the pastry cream.

6   Leave to chill for 30 minutes before using.

Chouquettes

C'EST CHOUETTE!

Makes approx. 25 chouquettes
Preparation time: 15 minutes
Cooking time: 15 minutes
Temperature: 160°C/320°F fan (Gas 4)

Choux dough:

75g water
50g milk
1 tsp orange-blossom water
1 tsp sea salt (or *fleur de sel*)
1 tbsp sugar
45g butter
75g flour (plain, all-purpose)
2 eggs

Topping:

2 tbsps pearl sugar (if you can't find pearl sugar, break up a few sugar lumps using a rolling pin)

Serve with hot chocolate, Earl Grey tea or an espresso

"It's a piece of cake", my daughter Julie triumphed, when she returned from a 9th birthday party pâtisserie workshop. She'd learned how to make choux pastry for chouquettes; her favourite part was using the piping bag. In French, I thought you could say "c'est du gâteau" for it's a piece of cake but in fact, the French say it (more familiarly) the other way around: "*Ce n'est pas du gâteau*", meaning it's *not* that easy. Well, it is: it's a piece of cake!

Chouquettes (pronounced "shookettes") are greedy bite-sized choux puffs – the smallest choux size – that are not filled but simply topped with pearl sugar. **If you haven't used a piping bag before then this is a great way to start out,** as the dough is thick enough for you to control the pressure of piping it out gradually. *C'est chouette!* (pronounced *shwet*) is a French description for something cute and sweet.

Parisians have been enjoying chouquettes since the 16th century. Apparently they were slightly perfumed with rosewater so, if you prefer rose, simply replace the orange blossom with rosewater in step 1 of the basic choux pastry recipe.

Chouquettes are sold by the kilo in French bakeries, as they can become compulsive eating. Because they only take half an hour to make and are delicious served warm and fresh from the oven, there's nothing like making them at home and recreating their delicate scent as if straight from a Paris *boulangerie*.

1   Make choux dough following the instructions on page 64 (except you're making a half quantity). Pipe out small heaps of about 3–4cm (1½") diameter onto a baking sheet lined with baking paper/parchment.

2   Brush each with a glaze of one egg yolk mixed with a tablespoon of water and sprinkle with pearl sugar. Bake in the oven for about 15 minutes at 160°C/320°F fan (Gas 4) until golden-light brown.

Waffles with Speedy Strawberry-Apricot Jam

GAUFRES ET CONFITURE EXPRESS

Makes approx. 6 waffles
Preparation time: 10 minutes
Cooking time: 30 minutes (for jam)

Choux dough:

75g water
50g milk
1 tsp sea salt
1 tbsp sugar
45g butter
75g flour (plain, all-purpose)
2 eggs

Jam (confiture):

200g fresh strawberries (or any other fruit)
4 apricots
100g jam sugar (sugar containing pectin)
1 tsp lemon juice
2 tbsps elderflower syrup (or any other syrup or alcohol of your choice for flavouring, although optional)

Serve with Darjeeling, Earl Grey or iced teas

If you have a waffle maker, leftover choux dough makes great round waffles or *gaufres*. I love to serve them with this handy fruity conserve that's quick and easy to make with any fresh fruit in season (otherwise you can use frozen). It keeps well in the fridge for up to 2 months, if you can wait that long.

1   Make choux dough as in the recipe on page 64 (except you'll be making a half quantity) or, preferably, if you have some leftover choux dough from another recipe simply use that.

2   Using the piping bag, push out spirals into a waffle maker and cook for a few minutes until puffed up and golden.

3   Clean and de-stalk the strawberries then place all the ingredients in a large saucepan and heat on medium until boiling.

4   Lower the heat and leave to simmer for about 15 minutes. Stir gently from time to time.

5   The express jam is ready when it thickens slightly. Mash up the strawberries with a potato masher or blitz with a hand blender. Decant into a couple of clean jam jars, leave to cool then seal them tightly with a lid. Store in the fridge.

Nun's Pops

PETS-DE-NONNE

Nut free

Makes approx. 25
Preparation time: 30 minutes
Cooking time: 4 minutes per batch

Choux dough:
75g water
50g milk
1 tsp salt
1 tbsp sugar
45g butter
75g flour (plain, all-purpose)
2 eggs
1 tbsp dark rum or orange blossom water

Light oil for deep-frying
Caster sugar (superfine sugar) or icing
sugar (confectioner's sugar) for coating

Serve with English breakfast or Oolong
teas

How can I phrase it delicately? The name "nun's pops" or "nun's puffs" is a bit of cheeky euphemism for a puff of wind that a nun might make. *Pets-de-nonne* are airy little choux-pastry puffs, flavoured with rum or orange-blossom water, that are quickly deep-fried in oil. The result is a light, sugar-coated crispy exterior with a soft inside that's full of air — and nothing remotely to do with cake pops.

Traditionally made at home, they ignite childhood memories for many French. My husband Antoine's family grew up eating these mini doughnuts in their hilltop village, where anything with a religious connotation is naturally taken seriously. Children can eat these even with the rum added, as the small amount of alcohol is cooked off but the beautiful fragrance lingers.

1 Preheat a deep fryer to 170°C/340°F.

2 Make choux dough as in the recipe on page 64 (except you are making a half quantity). Add the rum or orange-blossom water to flavour the dough and mix well.

3 Take a teaspoon of dough and use another teaspoon to slide it into the fryer, plunge a few balls at a time into the hot oil (or use a piping bag without a tip, squeeze out the mixture and cut off the dough with a knife or scissors after each 2cm/¾"). They'll sink to the bottom but quickly rise to the surface as they puff up and turn golden.

4 Fry for 3 to 4 minutes, turning them quickly so that they brown nicely all round. Drain the pops on kitchen paper to remove excess oil.

5 Continue frying more pops until you have finished the dough. Drain on kitchen paper.

6 When cooled slightly, roll the pops in caster (or icing) sugar.

7 Serve immediately. Dip them in warmed jam and it's top of the pops!

Cream Puffs
CHOUX À LA CRÈME

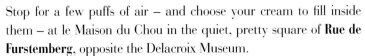

Nut free

Makes approx. 20
Preparation time: 40 minutes
Cooking time: 20 minutes
Cooling time: 30 minutes
Temperature: 160°C/320°F fan (Gas 4)

Choux dough:
75g water
50g milk
1 tsp sea salt (or *fleur de sel*)
1 tbsp sugar
45g butter
75g flour (plain, all-purpose)
2 eggs

Whipped mascarpone cream
200g whipping cream, chilled
100g mascarpone, chilled
1 tbsp sugar
½ tsp vanilla extract
3 tbsps icing sugar

8 strawberries, sliced (optional)

Serve with jasmine green tea

Stop for a few puffs of air – and choose your cream to fill inside them – at le Maison du Chou in the quiet, pretty square of **Rue de Furstemberg**, opposite the Delacroix Museum.

These cream puffs are given the Parisian touch with *craquelin* crumble topping (see page 70) but if you prefer without, simply dust your choux puffs liberally with icing sugar.

1   Preheat the oven to 160°C/320°F fan (Gas 4).

2   Make choux dough as in the recipe on page 64 (except you're making a half quantity).

3   Pipe out little puffs to about 4cm (1½") diameter using a plain tip of 12–14mm (½") onto a baking tray lined with baking paper/parchment and, if using, top each one with a 4cm disc of crumble topping (page 70).

4   Bake for 20 minutes.

5   Measure the cream in a bowl and chill in the fridge for about 30 minutes. Whip the cream and sugars using an electric whisk and when thickened, add the chilled mascarpone cream. Transfer to a piping bag with a serrated tip.

6   Cut off the tops of the choux puffs and press with your fingers to make a hollow in the bottom.

7   Pipe in the cream and press in a hidden strawberry slice then continue to pipe over the cream.

8   Place the choux hat on top then dust with icing sugar.

Strawberry Éclairs with Elderflower Cream

ÉCLAIRS À LA FRAISE ET FLEURS DE SUREAU

Nut free

Makes 8
Preparation time: 25 minutes
Cooking time: 35 minutes
Temperature: 160°C/320°F fan (Gas 4)

Choux dough:
75g water
50g milk
1 tsp sea salt (or *fleur de sel*)
1 tbsp sugar
45g butter
75g flour (plain, all-purpose)
2 eggs

24 strawberries

Pastry cream:
250g full-cream milk
1 vanilla pods (or beans)
3 egg yolks
30g caster sugar (superfine sugar)
20g cornflour (cornstarch)
1 tbsp elderflower syrup (I use Monin's)

Serve with elderflower cordial, or
Darjeeling or jasmine teas

One particular pastry chef, Christophe Adam, showcases his "genius éclairs" in **Rue Pavée**, between the Hotel de Ville and **Place de Vosges** in the **Marais**. Éclairs are not only easy to make but they're one of my favourite ways of serving up the best-tasting strawberries when they signal springtime. There's no need to make a glaze to coat the éclairs: just dust them with icing sugar. They are generously filled with a delicious pastry cream with a hint of elderflower, which goes beautifully with strawberries due to its floral notes and a nudge of lychee.

Try to find the shiniest, sweetest red berries in season, to appreciate the delicate taste of elderflower. In the French markets, the most popular, highly flavoursome strawberry varieties are *Gariguette*, *Mara des Bois* and *Charlotte*. If you can't get elderflower syrup why not use your favourite floral essence or try St Germaine elderflower liqueur.

1   Preheat the oven to 160°C/320°F fan (Gas 4).

2   Make choux dough as in the recipe on page 64 (except make a half quantity).

3   Using a piping bag with a 12mm (½") serrated tip, pipe out long éclairs to about 12cm (4¾") on baking trays covered with greaseproof/baking paper (or a silicone mat). Leave a good space between each of them, as they will spread out during baking.

4   Bake in the oven for 25–30 minutes until golden-medium brown. Leave éclairs to cool on a wire rack then cut the tops off horizontally.

5   Follow the pastry cream method on page 72, adding the elderflower syrup at the end of whisking. Immediately cover the pastry cream with cling film and, when cool, chill in the fridge for at least an hour.

6   Pipe out a generous line of cream on the bottom half of each éclair, top with four or five strawberries (if they're big, cut them in half). Crown with the éclair tops and powder with icing sugar. Chill until ready to serve.

Lemon and Verbena Mini Éclairs

ÉCLAIRS AU CITRON ET VERVEINE

Nut free

Makes approx. 12 mini éclairs
Preparation time: 25 minutes
Cooking time: 30 minutes
Temperature: 160°C/320°F fan (Gas 4)
Chilling time: 1 hour

Choux dough:
75g water
50g milk
1 tsp sea salt (or *fleur de sel*)
1 tbsp sugar
45g butter
75g flour (plain, all-purpose)
2 eggs

Lemon and verbena cream:
90g lemon juice (from approx. 3 lemons)
Finely grated zest of 2 unwaxed lemons
Branch of fresh verbena leaves; or 10
dried leaves (optional)
1 egg
2 egg yolks
10g cornflour (cornstarch)
50g caster sugar (superfine sugar)
125g butter, diced

Serve with Darjeeling, Ceylon or
gunpowder teas

Continuing our pastry walk in the Marais, there are yet more fruity éclairs to be tasted at Gérard Mulot on **Rue du Pas-de-la-Mule**. As the lemon season dovetails with the sweet debut of spring in March, there's nothing like applauding its finale before the capricious, erratic rains (known as *"Giboulées de mars"*, meaning April showers in March) bring the curtain down on winter. To celebrate the more-than-welcome arrival of sunny, fresh yellows in the Parisian parks, these dainty éclairs have just enough tartness in the filling, sweetened by a light sugar-dusting.

If you prefer a sticky fondant topping, mix together the juice of a lemon with three tablespoons of icing sugar.

The recipe is just a good without the verbena, so if you can't find any don't let that stop you making it.

1   Preheat oven to 160°C/320°F fan (Gas 4).

2   Make choux dough as in the recipe on page 64 (except you are making a half quantity). Using a serrated tip (12mm/½"), pipe out the dough to make éclairs about 8cm (3¼") in length on a baking sheet lined with baking paper/parchment or with a silicone mat.

3   Bake for about 20 minutes. Keep an eye on them after 15 minutes but keep the oven door closed. They should be golden but if they don't look completely cooked, bake them for a few minutes more.

4   Remove the eclairs from the baking sheet immediately and leave to cool on a wire rack.

LEMONS

It's so much easier to extract juice from lemons if they are at room temperature.

---

5 Put the lemon juice, zest, verbena leaves, egg, yolks, cornflour and sugar in a saucepan and, over a medium heat, whisk until the mixture foams then gradually thickens. Take off the heat and sieve the mixture to remove the zest and verbena leaves. Add the cold butter, whisking until smooth.

6 When cool, leave to chill in the fridge for an hour or, if in a hurry, for 30 minutes in the freezer.

7 Once cool, cut the éclairs tops off horizontally. Whisk the chilled lemon cream and transfer to a piping bag with either a plain or serrated 8–10mm (⅜") tip.

8 Generously pipe in the filling. Replace the éclair tops and lightly powder with icing sugar.

SUGARED FLOWERS

Sugared edible flowers are easy to make. Brush clean primroses or winter pansies with egg white, roll in granulated sugar and leave to dry in a cool place.

Speedy Lemon Cream
CRÈME DE CITRON EXPRESS

For busy gourmets, a speedy lemon cream is easy.

100g good quality lemon curd
100g of whipped cream

1 Fold the lemon curd into whipped cream (that has been whipped in a cold bowl).

2 Pipe into your choux pastries. Garnish with fresh strawberries or blueberries and dust with icing sugar (confectioner's sugar).

Chocolate Éclairs

ÉCLAIRS AU CHOCOLAT

Nut free

Makes approx. 8 éclairs
Preparation time: 40 minutes
Cooking time: 40 minutes
Temperature: 160°C/320°F fan (Gas 4)
Chilling time: 2 hours

Choux dough:
75g water
50g milk
1 tsp sea salt (or *fleur de sel*)
1 tbsp sugar
45g butter
75g flour (plain, all-purpose)
2 eggs

Chocolate cream:
200g milk
150g whipping cream
2 egg yolks
50g sugar
20g cornflour (cornstarch)
1 tsp vanilla extract
100g dark chocolate (at least 64% cocoa), broken into chunks

Chocolate glaze:
4g gelatine (2 x 2g sheets)
100g sugar
30g cocoa powder (100% unsweetened)
30g water
70g single cream

Serve with Assam, Earl Grey or Oolong teas

Éclairs can come in all kinds of fancy packaging as if decorated for a catwalk fashion show but there's nothing to beat a "plain" chocolate éclair. Apparently, following a recent French survey of chocolate éclairs in the "City of Light", Stohrer, the oldest pâtisserie in Paris came up trumps in **Rue Montorgueil**. In 1725 Nicolas Stohrer was pastry chef to Louis XV in **Versailles** and opened his own pastry shop there in 1730. He may have invented the *Baba au Rhum* (rum savarin cake) dessert but this institution knows a thing or two about éclairs too!

Looking up éclair in the French dictionary, you're given "a flash of lightning" as the translation. Well, given a bit of organisation, you can make these as quick as a flash. Appropriately, the word, éclair, falls in the dictionary under *éclat*, which refers to something dazzling or brilliantly shiny. A chocolate éclair's éclat comes from its glistening dark glaze (page 68).

1   Follow the instructions on page 68 for the chocolate glaze and set aside to chill in the fridge for at least 2 hours.

2   Preheat oven to 160°C/320°F fan (Gas 4).

3   Prepare the choux dough following the instructions on page 64 (except you're making a half quantity).

4   Using a 12mm (½") plain or serrated tip, pipe out éclairs (about 12cm/4¾" long) on a baking tray covered with baking paper/parchment (or a silicone mat). Leave a good space between each mound, as they will expand during baking.

5   Bake in the oven for 25–30 minutes.

6   Leave to cool on a wire rack.

7 For the chocolate cream, heat the milk and cream in a saucepan. Meanwhile, whisk the yolks and sugar in a bowl until light and creamy. Add the cornflour and vanilla extract and continue to whisk until smooth.

8 Gradually add the warm cream and return it to the pan, whisking constantly over a medium heat until thickened.

9 Remove from the heat, whisk in the chocolate bits until melted into a smooth, luxurious cream. Set aside and chill in the fridge for at least an hour.

10 Pierce three holes at the bottom of each éclair and, using a piping bag with a small tip, pipe in the chocolate cream.

11 Prepare the chocolate glaze following instructions on page 68. Dip the éclairs in the glaze. Chill in the fridge until ready to serve.

SAVING TIME

To save time, you can prepare the choux dough two days in advance. The glaze can be made either the day before – or even a week before – and frozen. The filling can be made the day before. On the day on which you wish to make your chocolate éclairs it will be possible to make them in a flash!

Coffee Éclairs

ÉCLAIRS AU CAFÉ-CRÈME

Nut free

Makes approx. 8 éclairs
Preparation time: 40 minutes
Cooking time: 40 minutes
Chilling time: 1 hour + 40 minutes
Temperature: 160°C/320°F fan (Gas 4)

Coffee pastry cream/crème légère
250ml full-cream milk
5g instant/soluble Arabica coffee powder
3 egg yolks
40g caster sugar (superfine sugar)
20g cornflour (cornstarch)
1 x 2g sheet of gelatine
80g whipping cream

Choux dough:
75g water
50g milk
1 tsp sea salt (or *fleur de sel*)
1 tbsp sugar
45g butter
75g flour (plain, all-purpose)
2 eggs

Glaze:
2g gelatine (1 x 2g sheet)
80g single cream
20g water
20g honey
120g white chocolate, broken into bits
1 tsp instant/soluble coffee

Serve with Assam or Yunnan teas

Coffee éclairs and chocolate éclairs are best buddies in the window in **Rue Montorgeuil**. You'll also often see them towering together in the form of a giant, tiered cone at Fauchon in **Place de la Madeleine**.

Crème légère (light pastry cream) is a luxurious pastry cream with added whipped cream and gelatine which is often used to fill millefeuilles. This coffee-cream filling also makes a delicious *latté millefeuille*.

1 Heat the milk and coffee powder in a saucepan over a low–medium heat. In a mixing bowl, whisk the yolks with the sugar and gradually add the cornflour. Whisk until light and creamy.

2 As soon as the milk starts to boil, pour half of the hot milk onto the yolk mix, whisk again and transfer back to the saucepan. Whisk continuously over a medium heat until thickened to a pastry cream consistency. Place cling film directly onto the pastry cream, set aside to cool before chilling in the fridge for at least an hour.

3 Preheat oven to 160°C/320°F fan (Gas 4). Prepare the choux dough following the instructions on page 64 (except you're making a half quantity).

4 Fill a piping bag with the dough, using a 12mm (½") tip. Pipe out éclairs (about 12cm/4¾" long) on a covered baking tray. Bake for 25–30 minutes.

5 Make pastry cream following the instructions on page 72 except adding instant coffee powder to the milk. Soak the gelatine in cold water for 15 minutes and mix with the warm pastry cream. Hand whisk the whipping cream till firm, then gradually fold into the gelatine and pastry cream. Chill for at least 40 minutes. Transfer to a piping bag with a 6–7mm (¼") tip. Pierce three small holes underneath each éclair and pipe in the coffee cream.

6 Follow the glaze recipe on page 68, adding 1 teaspoon of instant coffee powder to the cream in step one. Coat each éclair with the coffee glaze.

Pistachio and Cherry Kirsch Choux Puffs

CHOUX À LA PISTACHE ET GRIOTTE

Makes approx. 20 mini choux puffs
Preparation time: 40 minutes
Chilling time: 25 minutes
Cooking time: 1 hour
Temperature: 160°C/320°F fan (Gas 4)

Choux dough:

75g water
50g milk
1 tsp sea salt (or *fleur de sel*)
1 tbsp sugar
45g butter
75g flour (plain, all-purpose)
2 eggs

Pistachio cream:

250g milk
3 egg yolks
40g caster sugar (superfine sugar)
20g cornflour (cornstarch)
2 tsps pistachio paste (see page 98)
Few drops pistachio or almond extract
20g single cream

20 griotte cherries, or *Griottines*™

Glaze:

2g gelatine (1 x 2g sheet)
80g single cream
20g water
20g honey
120g white chocolate, broken into bits
1 tsp pistachio paste

Serve with Ceylon green or black teas

Invented by Italian chef Popelini in 1540, mini *choux à la crème* are achieving such popularity in Paris that designer choux shops are popping up with real teatime appeal, such as the Popelini boutique in **Rue Debelleyme**, a hidden gem in the trendy upper Marais.

This recipe's intense, hidden pistachio filling is deliciously fun with a topping of the simplest griotte cherry in syrup, or, for the adults, a *Griottine*™ (a cherry soaked in kirsch).

Just like macarons, choux puffs seduce us with cuteness. Their size and colour is as enticing as their *parfum* or flavour. If you prefer without glaze, sprinkle the tops with unsalted ground pistachios before baking and serve with a simple dusting of icing or confectioner's sugar, and why not place a griotte cherry inside instead.

1   Preheat oven to 160°C/320°F fan (Gas 4).

2   Prepare the choux dough following the instructions on page 64 (except you're making a half quantity). Pipe out heaps of about 4cm (1½") using a piping tip of 8–10mm (⅜"). Bake for 15–20 minutes. Place on a wire rack to cool completely.

3   Boil the milk with the pistachio paste in a saucepan.

4   In a mixing bowl, whisk the yolks with the sugar then add the cornflour. Whisk until light and creamy. Pour on the hot milk and transfer back to the saucepan, whisking continuously over a medium heat until bubbling and thickened.

5 Set aside and leave to cool. Place cling film onto the pastry cream and chill in the fridge for at least an hour.

6 Whisk the almond essence and cold cream into the pastry cream and transfer to a piping bag with a thin, plain tip (5–7mm/¼"). Piercing a hole in the bottom of each puff, pipe in the cream.

7 To glaze, follow the recipe on page 68 but add 1 teaspoon of pistachio paste (see below to make your own), which colours it naturally green. Dip the rounded tops of the puffs into the glaze.

8 Leave to set for a few minutes on a wire rack, then top each with a *Griottine*™ or a griotte cherry.

QUICK PISTACHIO PASTE

If you don't have pistachio paste, whizz 100g unsalted pistachios in a grinder. Mix together with 25g ground almonds, 50g sugar, 2 drops of pistachio (or almond) essence and a tablespoon of water. The paste can keep in the fridge for up to a month.

CHOCOLATE, PISTACHIO AND CHERRY

Use the chocolate glaze recipe on page 68, since chocolate added to pistachio and griotte cherries is heaven! Even simpler, fill éclairs with the pistachio cream and top with fresh cherries.

Religieuse Rose

RELIGIEUSE À LA ROSE

Nut free
Makes 8
Preparation time: 90 minutes
Cooking time: 65 minutes
Temperature: 160°C/320°F fan (Gas 4)

Choux dough:

150g water
100g milk
1 tsp sea salt (or *fleur de sel*)
2 tbsps sugar
90g butter
150g flour (plain, all-purpose)
4 eggs

Rose pastry cream:

500g full-cream milk
15g rosewater (see page 30)
6 egg yolks
40g cornflour (cornstarch)
80g sugar

Lychee cream:

60g whipping cream (32–35%)
15g lychee syrup (Monin)
40g sugar
125g (½ tub) mascarpone, chilled

Glaze:

2g gelatine (1 x 2g sheet)
80g single cream
20g water
20g honey
120g white chocolate, broken into bits
1 tsp rosewater (see page 30)
Pinch of pink colouring

8 fresh raspberries

Serve with Darjeeling tea

There's a particular flavour of pastry that has tourists and Parisians braving the longest queues in Paris in June, especially around Ladurée and Pierre Hermé in **Rue Bonaparte**. Inspired by the *Ispahan* Iranian rose, blushing pink macarons are flavoured with rose and lychee cream and decorated with raspberries. Pastry chefs around Paris have also adopted this amazing flavour-combination for other pastries such as the éclair and the *religieuse*.

What is a religieuse? It's a nun, but somehow the name was given to a pastry! It was invented by Frascati, an Italian pastry chef, in Paris in 1856. It uses the same methods of preparation as a chocolate or coffee éclair but is presented differently: a large choux bun as a base with a smaller choux bun on top, filled with pastry cream, coated with a shiny glaze and finished off with a ruffled collar to stick them together.

The decorative ruffle between the choux puffs is traditionally made with a technical French buttercream (*crème au beurre*) but instead, many French chefs opt for mascarpone cream, which is light and easy to make. You can substitute lychee for rose syrup.

1   Preheat the oven to 160°C/320°F fan (Gas 4).

2   Prepare the choux dough following the instructions on page 64, then pipe out eight large choux puffs (about 5cm/2" diameter) using a 12–14mm (½") plain tip on parchment paper or a silicone mat on a baking tray. Bake for 25 minutes. On another lined baking tray, pipe out eight small choux puffs (about 2cm/¾" diameter) and bake for 15 minutes. Once baked, remove from the oven and cool on a wire rack.

> **LARGE CHOUX PUFFS**
> For the larger-bottom choux puffs, it will be easier using a bigger piping nozzle of around 14–16mm (⅝").

3 For the rose pastry cream, follow the instructions on page 72 except add rosewater to the milk. Once thickened, place cling film directly on top of the pastry cream and leave to cool. Chill in the fridge for an hour.

4 Make the mascarpone cream: whisk the cream, then add the syrup and gradually add the chilled mascarpone until the cream is stiff. Transfer to a piping

VARIATION

To make a rose, raspberry and lychee éclair, fill your éclairs with the rose cream and fill each raspberry cavity with the lychee cream.

bag with a small star or flower nozzle to decorate later and chill until needed.

5 Using a sharp knife, pierce a hole in the bottom of the choux puffs and pipe in the rose cream.

6 To glaze: follow the recipe on page 68, adding a little pink colouring, and a few drops of rosewater. Dip the rounded tops of the choux buns into the rose glaze.

7 Stick the small choux bun on top of the bigger one and crown it with a raspberry on top. Pipe out the mascarpone cream as a collar between the head and the body to ensure it stays straight.

8 Leave to chill in the fridge and eat fresh on the same day.

6ᵉ Arrᵗ

RUE BONAPARTE

1769 - 1821 NAPOLÉON BONAPARTE

FRENCH TARTLETS
As Easy as Meringue Pie

Some teatime chic to showcase seasonal delights

The other day, when I gave a chocolate crumble puff tartlet to my husband's Great Aunt Raymonde (she's a spritely and beautiful 94-year-old French lady, who still wears mascara and always has immaculate hair), she looked at me with her dazzling eyes and said, *"Mon Dieu! C'est pour moi? Mais ce n'est pas de la tarte."*

"Yes, it *is* a tart," I answered, confused.

"Non," she replied, "'it's not the tart'. It's an expression meaning that it can't be that easy to make."

Well it *is* easy. Or it's not difficult; whatever you prefer. The French are just so clever at tarts. The best bases are not too sweet and have that hint of salt to them. They showcase their contents to the full, whether it's seasonally fresh and fruity, topped with billowing meringue, decadent chocolate, oozing with sticky caramel, or full of crunchy, crazy nuttiness. Somehow, individual tartlets have that teatime chic. As the chocolate and caramel tartlets are even better next day, they are perfect for taking into work in a cake box to impress the boss at teatime.

The beauty of making tartlets rather than a larger tart is that there's no need to blind bake the base first so, as a *lazy gourmet*, that's another step avoided. I use either 10cm (4") diameter non-stick tartlet moulds or classic tartlet rings.

Sweet Pastry
PÂTÉ SUCRÉE

Makes 500g pastry; 8 tartlets or 1 large
tart
Preparation time: 10 minutes
Chilling/resting time: 1 hour
Cooking time: 10–15 minutes (20 mins
for a large tart)
Temperature: 160°C/320°F fan (Gas 4)

125g butter, softened, at room
temperature
75g icing sugar (confectioner's sugar)
½ tsp salt
1 egg
½ tsp vanilla extract (optional)
240g plain flour (all-purpose flour),
sifted

This sweet pastry is slightly crispy and ideal for your fruity tarts, as it tends to not get a soggy bottom. It also has less butter than shortcrust pastry (*pâté sablée*) so it's easier to work with. If you love a more crumbly shortbread texture to accompany your tea, then try the *diamant* biscuits on page 40.

Many pastry chefs add nuts to their pastry dough, though I prefer to keep it plain. For nutty pastry use 230g flour and 20g ground almonds. The best flour to use for tartlets is the finest that you can find, that doesn't produce lumps. In France, I use *farine fluide* (type 45). Plain, all-purpose flour (type 55) is still good – just ensure that you sift before baking. You can make sweet pastry mixing the ingredients by hand (using cold butter) but a stand mixer is so much quicker and hassle-free.

The recipe makes eight tartlets (10cm/4" diameter). Any leftover (uncooked) pastry can be stored in the fridge for up to three days and can also be frozen (just defrost the pastry overnight). I sometimes just use half the amount: cut the pastry in two, wrap separately in cling film, use one and freeze one.

1   Using a stand mixer with a paddle beater, slowly mix the butter, sugar and salt until pale and creamy. Just for a few seconds, gradually add the other ingredients until the dough is well mixed, then stop.

2   Form the dough into a ball, wrap in cling film and chill in the fridge for at least an hour.

3 Remove from the fridge. Preheat the oven to 160°C/320°F fan (Gas 4).

4 Roll out the pastry to 3–4mm (⅛–³⁄₁₆") thickness using a rolling pin turning regularly on a lightly floured surface (not too much flour or it will affect your pastry).

5 Using a round scone cutter (or a drinking glass) that is 1–2cm (¾") diameter larger than your tartlet moulds, cut out each round; or cut out a round that is 2cm (¾") bigger than the tartlet mould.

VARIATIONS

For chocolate pastry, add 20g of unsweetened cocoa powder.

For an aromatic pastry add a teaspoon of pumpkin spice or gingerbread spice.

6 Gently press into each tartlet mould, trimming off excess pastry with your fingers or roll over the edges with a rolling pin.

7 Prick the pastry all over with a fork. For tartlets there is no need to blind bake your pastry.

LARGER TARTS

For larger tarts, cover with baking parchment (cut to size – I re-use the same one over a couple of baking sessions for convenience) and fill with ceramic baking "beans", washed coins, rice or dried beans to blind bake the pastry.

8 For tartlets bake for 10–15 minutes (I've found that 12 minutes is good; chocolate tartlets will need a bit longer, about 15 minutes). If making a large tart, bake for 15 minutes, remove baking paper and beans and bake for another 5–10 minutes or until the pastry is golden.

9 Leave to cool, remove from the moulds and set aside.

FILLINGS

Fill with the flavoured pastry cream of your choice and top with whatever fruits are in season.

Caramel, Walnut and Maple Tartlets

TARTELETTES AU CARAMEL, NOIX ET SIROP D'ÉRABLE

Makes 8 tartlets
Preparation time: 20 minutes
Chilling time: 2 hours
Cooking time: 20 minutes
Temperature: 160°C/320°F fan (Gas 4)

Sweet pastry:

125g butter, softened, at room temperature
75g icing sugar (confectioner's sugar)
½ tsp salt
1 egg
½ tsp vanilla extract (optional)
240g plain flour (all-purpose flour), sifted

Filling:

50g walnuts (or a mixture of other nuts)
220g granulated sugar
90g single cream (hot – important)
75g maple syrup
50g butter, soft
½ tsp sea salt (or *fleur de sel*)

Serve with Ceylon green or black, or Assam teas

I love **Rue du Bac**. Who could ask for more than a street in Paris with a handful of the haute pâtisseries lined up for you to taste plenty of sticky caramel treats in all sorts of guises? As if five of the top pastry shops weren't enough, around the corner there's also Dalloyau on **Rue de Grenelle** and Victor & Hugo on **Boulevard Raspail**.

This recipe is one that you can make the day before and tastes even better the next day. Make these tartlets on Sunday and surprise your colleagues with them at teatime on Monday!

1   Follow the sweet pastry recipe on pages 106–9 and cut out eight tartlets. Bake the tartlets for 10–15 minutes at 160°C/320°F fan (Gas 4). Allow to cool, remove from their moulds and set aside.

2   Chop the walnuts finely using a sharp knife or whizz them up in a food processor until fine but not powder.

3   Heat the sugar on a medium heat in a saucepan. Once it starts to melt (after about 3 minutes), stir gently with a long wooden spoon and leave the sugar to continue to melt. Turn down the heat to low and stir until the sugar has completely melted and forms a light golden caramel.

4   Heat the single cream and maple syrup in another pan until almost boiling (or use the microwave for no more than a minute). Turn down the heat as low as possible and add the hot maple cream to the caramel, stirring well.

5   Take off the heat, stirring in the butter until melted, and stir in the finely chopped walnuts and the sea salt.

6   Pour immediately into the cooled tartlet cases and leave to cool for an hour.

TOASTED NUTS

Toast a larger quantity of walnuts and when cool, keep in a sealed jar. It's a handy, last-minute healthy sprinkle on many chocolate and coffee desserts.

Double Chocolate Tartlets

TARTELETTES AU CHOCOLAT

Makes 8 tartlets
Preparation time: 25 minutes
Cooking time: 30 minutes
Chilling time: 1 hour 30 minutes
Temperature: 160°C/320°F fan (Gas 4)

Chocolate pastry cases:

125g butter, at room temperature

75g icing sugar (confectioner's sugar)

½ tsp salt

1 egg

½ tsp vanilla extract (optional)

240g plain flour all-purpose), sifted

20g unsweetened cocoa powder

Ganache filling:

160g dark cooking chocolate

80g milk chocolate

230g single cream

1 tsp vanilla extract

Serve with a pot of Grand Yunnan, rooibos tea or, if you like smoky teas, lapsang souchong

Having visited **Sacré-Coeur** and dodged past the giant rolls of colourful fabrics at the bottom of **Montmartre's** bustling hill, head to **Rue des Martyrs** to escape the summer crowds. The further south of **Pigalle** (SoPi) you walk towards the 9th district, the more tempting pastry and chocolate boutiques appear. One of my favourites is Sébastian Gaudard and just across the road is a little chocolate shop and yet more pastries at Arnaud Delmontel.

The beauty of these chocolate tartlets is that the variations are endless. Serve them plain with a simple dusting of unsweetened Belgian cocoa powder, or spoon a tablespoon of jam on the bases before pouring on the ganache and topping with fruits.

1   Follow the sweet pastry recipe on pages 106–9, adding 20g unsweetened cocoa, and cut out eight tartlets. Bake the tartlets for 10–15 minutes at 160°C/320°F fan (Gas 4). Allow to cool, and remove from their moulds.

2   To make the ganache filling, break the chocolate into chunks in a bowl. Heat the cream with the vanilla extract in a saucepan until nearly boiling. Pour over half of the hot cream directly into the bowl of chocolate.

3   Stir using a wooden spoon and combine until the ganache is smooth. Top with the rest of the hot cream and stir until completely melted and silky.

4   Pour the hot ganache into each tartlet and top with a cherry, berries or keep plain. Leave to chill in the fridge for at least an hour to set. Take the tartlets out of the fridge 30 minutes before eating.

VARIATIONS

Infuse the seeds of 12 cardamom pods and a teaspoon of grated ginger in the cream while making the ganache and serve with a mango and passion fruit salad.

Why not spread the bases with thick cut marmalade and top with Cape gooseberries?

Passion Fruit and Lemon Meringue Tartlets

TARTELETTES AU FRUIT DE LA PASSION ET CITRON MERINGUÉE

Nut free

Makes 8 tartlets
Preparation time: 25 minutes
Cooking time: 20 minutes
Chilling time: 2 hours
Temperature: 160°C/320°F fan (Gas 4),
then 200°C (400°F, Gas 7)

One quantity sweet pastry (page 106):
125g butter, at room temperature
75g icing sugar (confectioner's sugar)
½ tsp salt
1 egg
½ tsp vanilla extract (optional)
240g plain flour (all-purpose), sifted

Filling:
Zest of an unwaxed lemon
Juice of 2 passion fruits and 1–2 lemons
(100g fresh juice)
100g sugar
2 eggs
90g cold butter, cut into chunks
1 x 2g sheet of gelatine

Meringue topping:
60g egg whites (approx. 2 egg whites)
90g sugar (normal sugar, not caster/
super-fine)

Serve with Ceylon or gunpowder teas

A lemon meringue tart is my kind of sweet treat since it's not really that sweet. It's quite tart, just enough to give that zinging feeling (*les peps*) as you bite through the clouds of meringue into the citrus, with a final hint of salt in the pastry.

Sublime tangy tarts can be had in **Rue de Turenne**, **Rue du Bac**, and also in **Rue de Seine** at Arnaud Lahrer's MOF pâtisserie. An MOF, or *Meilleur Ouvrier de France*, is the Olympian of French craftsmen, the best in their field. As from the age of 23, candidates go before a jury every four years to battle it out to prove how they are the best in the land. Those that achieve MOF status have the title for life and you'll see them – quite rightly – showing it off in their shop fronts. If you've got it, flaunt it!

I've added passion fruit to these tartlets, adding an extra zingy-ness which balances well with the sweet topping of meringue. If you don't top them with the meringue and serve them as a plain tart, to balance the acidity add another 50g sugar to the fruity cream and finish off with candied lemon peel for garnish.

1 Follow the sweet pastry recipe on pages 106–9 and cut out eight tartlets. Bake the tartlets for 10–15 minutes at 160°C/320°F fan (Gas 4). Allow to cool, remove from their moulds and set aside.

2 Soak the gelatine in cold water for 10 minutes and zest the lemon.

3 Strain the juice of two passion fruits using a sieve to remove all the seeds and make up to 100g by adding the juice of 1–2 lemons.

4 In a saucepan, whisk together the passion fruit-lemon juice with the sugar, zest and eggs over a medium heat until the sauce boils, bubbles and thickens.

5 Strain to remove the zest. Take off the heat and whisk in the butter and the gelatine (squeezed of excess water.)

6 Pour directly into the tartlet shells and place them in the fridge until ready to serve.

7 To appreciate them at their best, remove from the fridge 10 minutes before serving.

MERINGUE

1 Whisk the egg whites at medium-high speed with an electric mixer in either a glass or metallic bowl. Just as they start to froth up, gradually add the sugar. Increase to a high speed, continuing with the sugar until the meringue forms strong, glossy, stiff peaks.

2 Spoon (or transfer to a piping bag with a large serrated or plain tip and pipe out) the meringue on top of each tartlet, spreading it as much as possible over the top. If not piping, using the back of the spoon, lift parts of the meringue up into little cones (this reminds me of making cone shapes with shampoo foam during children's bath time!) for decoration.

3 Bake in a very hot oven (200°C, 400°F, Gas 7) for about 5 minutes. Alternatively, brown with a culinary blowtorch.

4 Remove and chill until ready to serve.

VARIATIONS

If you prefer to use just lemon rather than with the passion fruit, then you'll need about three lemons to make up 100g juice. Serve without meringue, topped with fruit instead and make with chocolate pastry, see picture on opposite page, top.

MERINGUE

For meringue, if your egg whites are aged for a couple of days and at room temperature, there's no need to use any salt, lemon or cream of tartare. This recipe uses French meringue, a quick method, which also means you'll need to act quickly as soon as it's whipped up. Don't answer the phone and leave the meringue on the counter for a few minutes – top the tartlets *tout de suite*!

Strawberry and Pistachio Tartlets

TARTELETTES À LA FRAISE ET PISTACHE

Makes 8 tartlets
Preparation time: 25 minutes
Cooking time: 20 minutes
Temperature: 160°C/320°F fan (Gas 4)
Chilling time: 1 hour

Sweet pastry:

125g butter, at room temperature
75g icing sugar (confectioner's sugar)
½ tsp salt
1 egg
½ tsp vanilla extract (optional)
240g plain flour (all-purpose), sifted

Pistachio pastry cream:

250g milk
3 egg yolks
40g caster sugar (superfine sugar)
20g cornflour (cornstarch)
2 tsps pistachio paste (see page 98)
Few drops pistachio or almond extract
20g single cream

Garnish:

8 large strawberries

Serve with a pot of Ceylon or Darjeeling tea

I first tasted this divine yet simple combination of pistachio cream and strawberry while gazing up at the ornate Tiepolo ceiling of the Jacquemart-André Museum's café-tea room on **Boulevard Hausseman**. Imagining the bird's eye view looking down from the ceiling: at the cultured museum-goers taking a relaxing break on red velvet upholstered golden chairs, sipping on tea or champagne while surrounded by Belgian tapestries and fresh floral displays. Perhaps the best view is of the array of choices on the glass-topped pastry trolley (supplied by Stohrer, the oldest Parisian pâtisserie) and its accompanying shiny silver tongs.

1   Follow the sweet pastry recipe on pages 106–9, roll out the pastry and cut out eight tartlets. Bake the tartlets for 10–15 minutes at 160°C/320°F fan (Gas 4). Allow to cool, remove from their moulds and set aside.

2   Make the pistachio pastry cream filling following instructions on page 74. Fill the eight tartlet bases with the pastry cream.

3 To make the strawberry fan garnish: stand the strawberry on its green stem on the table. Lay a wooden spoon behind it, then lean the strawberry against the stem of the spoon, as you can see in the picture below. Cut down through the strawberry with a sharp knife in thin slices, letting the knife land on the stem of the spoon, so as to cut only $^4/_5$ of the way through the fruit. Fan out the strawberry with your fingertips and garnish. It's as easy as pie!

VARIATIONS

There are countless fruity tartlet versions you can make by mixing and matching flavoured pastry creams to match your favourite fruits.

Chocolate pastry base for a chocolate-pistachio tartlet (see page 108) and top with fresh cherries, see picture on opposite page.
Elderflower pastry cream (follow recipe on page 74) topped with a fanned strawberry.
Rose pastry cream (see page 74), topped with raspberries and lychees.

Fast Fig, Almond and Lavender Tart

TARTE AUX FIGUES, AMANDES ET LAVANDE

Preparation time: 25 minutes
Baking time: 20 minutes
Temperature: 180°C/360°F fan (Gas 6)

250g all-butter, ready-made, or ready-rolled, puff pastry
12–15 purple plump figs (ripe but firm enough to cut neatly)
120g ground almonds (almond flour)
3 tbsps runny lavender honey
1 egg
2 tbsps dark rum (or orange blossom water)
Dried lavender flowers or flaked almonds (optional, for decoration)

Serve with a pot of Oolong orange blossom tea

They can say what they like; I *do* give a fig: fig season is far too short. This is also a short recipe that's quick and easy. What I love about this tart is its taste and simplicity with few ingredients, letting the figs shine through. The best part for us lazy gourmets is that it's made using ready-made puff pastry!

At the farmers' markets in Paris, these plump purple figs are packaged like jewels, individually nested in their crates, begging customers to squeeze them for ripeness. Pick figs that are ripe but firm enough to the touch; that way it will be easier to cut them into thin slices.

For that extra taste of France, scatter dried lavender flowers over the tart once it comes out of the oven, or sprinkle on a few flaked almonds. To make the fig season last a bit longer, you can freeze the tart for up to a month.

If you're looking for tarts (or macarons) bursting with fruit to accompany your pot of tea, head to Gérard Mulot's cosy little tea room in **Rue des Quatre-Vents**, where the pastries are brought from their pâtisserie next door, on the corner of **Rue Lobineau** and **Rue de Seine**.

1 Roll out the ready-made puff pastry to a depth of approximately 5mm (¼") and cut into a dinner-plate sized round.

2 Place on a baking sheet lined with greaseproof baking paper. Prick the pastry with a fork and score a border 1cm (⅜") in from the edge using the sharp tip of a knife (don't cut all the way through). Place in the fridge for 20 minutes. Preheat the oven to 180°C/360°F fan (Gas 6).

3 Wash, dry and cut the figs finely, using a good sharp knife.

4 Beat the egg and honey with a whisk in a bowl until light and creamy. Add the ground almonds and the dark rum. Using a spatula, spread the mix on the pastry.

5 Place the figs in rounds on the pastry. Bake in the oven at 180°C/360°F fan (Gas 6) for about 20 minutes.

Pistachio and Cherry King Cake
GALETTE DES ROIS À LA PISTACHE ET GRIOTTE

Serves 6–8
Preparation time: 20 minutes
Chilling time: 30 minutes
Cooking time: 30 minutes
Temperature: 160°C/320°F fan (Gas 4)

Almond cream filling:
140g butter, softened
100g ground almonds (almond flour)
50g ground pistachios (unsalted)
130g caster sugar (superfine sugar)
2 eggs
1 tbsp cornflour (cornstarch)
2 tbsps kirsch
1 tbsp pistachio paste (or 1 tsp almond extract)

12 large griotte cherries in syrup (or dried cherries)

Pastry:
600g ready-made puff pastry (pure butter) rolled out to 5mm (¼") and cut into 2 circles of the same size

To glaze:
1 egg yolk
1 tbsp milk

Decoration:
1 fève or trinket
1 paper crown

Serve with Normandy cider or any other kind of off-dry bubbly

Trust the French to boost the morale when the Christmas decorations come down and the New Year festivities are over. On January 6th, with the arrival of Epiphany (or Twelfth Night), celebrations continue with sweet galettes.

The *galette des rois* (or king's cake) is traditionally served at Epiphany and is said to have taken its name from the three wise men. You'll find galettes on display in all the French pâtisseries at the start of the year – although you can find them increasingly before Christmas too – much like finding Easter eggs in February.

The galette des rois is not a cake as such but more of a giant puff pastry sandwich filled with frangipane (almond cream added to pastry cream), or, in this case, a simple almond cream with a touch of rum. The most exciting part for children is that the galette includes a *fève* or trinket hidden inside. There's even a French children's song that we used to sing to our girls when they were toddlers: *"J'aime la galette, savez-vous comment? Quand elle est bien faite, avec du beurre dedans; tra-la-la…"*. Yes, no buts, it has to be made with butter!

So that there's no cheating as to who gets the trinket when cutting the galette, tradition is that the youngest person in the room sits under the table and shouts out one by one each person's name in the room as the galette is cut by an "older and wiser" person above. The person who gets the slice with the trinket nestling inside wears the crown and is then King (or Queen) for the day. Sometimes in the chic pâtisseries, you're given two crowns. That way a King can choose a Queen, and vice versa.

On finding the fève again this year, my youngest daughter, Lucie, took one look at her Galette King and said, "Don't worry, Papa: I'll do what Napoleon did and just crown myself!"

1 Cream the butter in a large bowl then gradually add all the other almond cream filling ingredients and mix together well till smooth.

2 Place the first pastry circle on a baking sheet covered with baking parchment. Spread the almond cream mix evenly on top, leaving a space of 3cm (1¼") as a border (otherwise the yolk will stop the pastry from rising correctly.)

3 Insert the porcelain trinket well into the almond cream towards the edge of the galette (otherwise the galette cutter will keep hitting the trinket and you'll not be that popular!) Add the cherries.

4 Brush the yolk around the border then place the second puff pastry circle carefully on top, pressing down at the edge of the filling border to ensure there are no air bubbles. You'll be left with the top circle smaller than the bottom so, using a sharp knife, cut off the surplus pastry and stick it to the outside edge, sealing thoroughly all the way around the galette.

5 Now go around the galette's border and, using the blunt side of a knife and keeping it straight, make tiny indentations: either criss-cross back and forward or form a pretty pattern by pushing in at 3cm (1¼") intervals (see diagram).

6 Brush the top of the pastry with a glaze of egg yolk and milk.

7 For best results, leave to chill in the fridge for 30 minutes. This will help to keep the decoration you're about to do!

8 Preheat the oven to 160°C/320°F fan (Gas 4).

9 Again, using the blunt side of a knife, carefully score

a sun-ray pattern by cutting gently into the pastry, but not too much that you cut the pastry. Glaze again with the egg yolk then pierce four or five holes into the pastry to let any air escape for an even rise.

10 Bake in the oven for 30 minutes at 160°C/320°F fan (Gas 4). [Optional: brush with syrup (boil 2 tablespoons sugar with 1 tablespoon water or use a store-bought syrup) to add a refined, glossy finish for that pâtisserie-window look!] Cool for about 10 minutes and serve warm.

VARIATIONS

Chocolate-hazelnut-pear galette:
Replace the ground pistachios with ground hazelnuts, replace the pistachio paste with 80g grated dark chocolate and top with 2 sliced medium pears.

Matcha green tea and candied chestnut:
Replace the pistachios with more ground almonds, the Kirsch with rum, add 1 tablespoon of matcha green tea and replace the cherries with 2 candied chestnuts, broken into pieces. (With a bow to Japanese pastry inspiration in Paris!)

Orange: Almond paste with orange blossom water in place of the kirsch and replace cherries with bits of candied orange peel.

Rose and quince: Almond paste with rose water in place of rum or kirsch and add sliced poached quinces or pears.

MILLEFEUILLES
A Thousand Leaves

Looks difficult? The hardest part is pronouncing it!

The pâtisserie Seugnot, previously in **Rue du Bac**, produced these famous "thousand-leaf" pastries from 1867. Today, the *millefeuille* is a classic that has been copied all over Paris, layer by lip-smacking layer. It's a toasted, flaky alignment of puff-pastry layers, filled with vanilla pastry cream and given a light dusting of icing sugar to complete this prestigious stack of temptation. As for a thousand leaves ... I've never taken the time to count them but one of the pâtisseries in vogue claims to have 2000 layers.

With so many flaky layers to dive into, just try and eat this without making a decadent mess while enjoying its creamy taste and smooth, crispy textures.

Why did I shy away from the millefeuille for so long? "Cheating" with ready-made puff pastry makes it simplicity itself. Believe me, the hardest part of this recipe is pronouncing it in French!

The most important tip in making the classic, flat pastry layers is to place the pastry rectangles or discs on a baking sheet, lined with baking paper or parchment, cover with another sheet of baking paper and top with another baking sheet. This stops the pastry from rising in the oven. The top layers of each millefeuille are quickly caramelised under the grill for that shiny, extra-glossy look and given a final light dusting of icing/confectioner's sugar. Each layer is filled with pastry cream, often with added berries, but not filled too much that the pastry towers are too high. Press each layer down gently to touch the cream.

The French often use a *crème légère* or *crème diplomate* for millefeuilles. It's chilled pastry cream with added whipped cream and set beautifully with gelatine (for vegetarians, replace the 2g sheet of gelatine with ½ tsp agar-agar powder). In the **Vanilla Millefeuille for Sunday** recipe, for those of you who are not rum fans, replace the filling with the light coffee pastry cream from page 94 to enjoy *Latte Millefeuilles* (see picture opposite).

Millefeuilles are best eaten fresh. If you make them in advance, serve within two hours otherwise they will turn upsettingly soggy. To risk disappointment, I prepare the pastry layers in advance earlier in the afternoon, have the cream ready in its piping bag with tip and serve them at the last minute while the kettle is boiling.

Vanilla Millefeuille for Sunday

MILLEFEUILLE DU DIMANCHE

Nut free

Makes 8
Preparation time: 25 minutes
Chilling time: 1 hour
Cooking time: 30 minutes
Temperature: 160°C/320°F fan (Gas 4)

Vanilla and rum pastry cream:
500g milk
2 vanilla pods/beans
6 egg yolks
80g sugar
50g cornflour (cornstarch)
2 tbsps dark rum

Pastry:
500g pure-butter puff pastry (or 2 x
250g-packets ready-rolled puff pastry)
Icing/confectioner's sugar

Serve with Ceylon or Keemun tea

This is not-so-plain vanilla if you use good quality, sticky and fat vanilla pods/beans from Madagascar, which are intensely powerful and full of flavour.

Our local pâtissier is renowned for his vanilla *millefeuilles*. He traditionally makes them for clients only on a Sunday and the impatient queue drifting over from the local market is enough to warrant assistance from the traffic gendarmes. It's not so much the vanilla that makes them famous with the older clientèle, it's the rum that packs a particular punch that calls for a blissful dimanche *sieste*, or afternoon nap. Perhaps it's also an ideal dessert night-cap! If you happen to be around the **Hotel de Ville** and **Marais** area, then a walk up to Jacques Genin's tea salon in **Rue de Turenne** is a must for one of the best millefeuilles in Paris. The boutique resembles more of a pastry museum!

This recipe perhaps may look complicated, but with ready-made pastry it's easy to put this together.

1   Preheat the oven to 160°C/320°F fan (Gas 4).

2   Make pastry cream according to the method on page 72, whisk in the 2 tablespoons of rum at the end of cooking. Cover with cling film and chill in the fridge for at least an hour.

3   If not already pre-rolled, roll out the pastry to a 5mm (¼") thickness. Cut out 24 rectangles of puff pastry about 10cm x 5cm (4" x 2"). You will need three per person. For perfectionists, don't worry if they're not completely straight, as you can trim the sides at the end, if necessary.

4   Place each rectangle on a baking sheet lined with baking parchment. Place another sheet of baking parchment over them and top with another baking sheet to stop the pastry from puffing up too much in the oven.

5   Bake in the oven for 15 minutes. Remove the rectangles and place on a wire rack to cool.

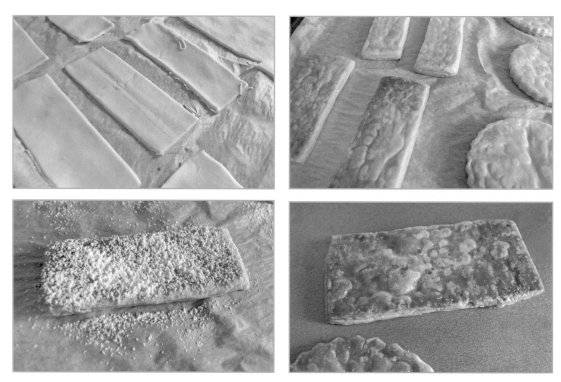

6 Place eight of the rectangles on a baking tray (without the baking paper), dust them with icing sugar, place under a grill for a few seconds to caramelise (no longer than a minute – keep your eye on them!), for an extra sticky gourmet look to top each millefeuille.

7 Remove and leave to cool. At this point, you can trim the sides with a sharp knife, so that you can see the crisp puff pastry layers.

8 Whisk the chilled pastry cream and transfer to a piping bag with a 10–12mm (½") plain tip. Pipe out blobs onto each rectangle base, cover with another pastry layer, pipe out more cream, then top with the final, caramelised rectangle.

9 Dust the tops of each millefeuille with icing sugar (I simply placed a piece of paper over the top to create this icing sugar pattern). Chill in the fridge.

10 Serve within 2 hours, as these are best eaten fresh.

VARIATION
Add a few raspberries to each layer and you have a "Napoleon" pastry.

Mint and Strawberry Millefeuille

MILLEFEUILLE À LA MENTHE ET AUX FRAISES

Nut free

Serves 10
Preparation time: 20 minutes (30 minutes infusion)
Chilling time: 1 hour 30 minutes
Cooking time: 15 minutes
Temperature: 160°C/320°F fan (Gas 4)

Mint leaves from 1 large branch
500ml full-cream milk
6 egg yolks
70g sugar
50g cornflour (cornstarch)
200ml whipping cream (at least 33% butterfat)
2 x 2g sheets of gelatine
500g pure-butter puff pastry (or 2 x 250g packets ready-rolled puff pastry)
Strawberries

Serve with mint tea

During the *canicules* or heat waves of the last few Parisian summers, the glacial taste of refreshing mint has been a welcome treat. One of the most natural ruby-red luxuries is seeing dainty wild or alpine strawberries (*fraises des bois* – literally, wild woodland strawberries) sit in their prized punnets at the market like glistening jewels (at the price, you'd think they were beaded together as a necklace in one of the high-end jewellers in **Place Vendôme**!). Popping one in the mouth, though, is like relishing the most prized sweet *bonbon*.

You can prepare the light mint cream the day before, just keep chilled in the fridge. The puff pastry layers can be prepared in advance, earlier in the day. Just assemble before needed. Wild strawberries are not essential, slices of standard-size strawberries will be fine.

1   Wash and dry the mint leaves.

2   Boil the milk with the mint leaves, take off the heat and leave the leaves to infuse for 30 minutes with a lid on the pot.

3   Beat together the egg yolks and sugar until light and creamy, then whisk in the cornflour.

4 Remove the leaves from the milk with a slotted spoon then beat half of the milk into the egg mixture. Transfer this to the milk and over a medium heat, whisk for about 5 minutes until the mixture thickens.

5 Cover this custard mixture with cling film, so that no skin forms on top, and set it aside to cool.

6 Place a glass bowl in the freezer.

7 Soak gelatine in water for 10 minutes.

8 Whip the cream with an electric mixer in the cold bowl until you have whipped cream (chantilly cream). Take a little pastry cream and reheat it in the microwave for a few seconds and add the gelatine. Fold into the pastry cream and chill for another 30 minutes.

9 Cut small rounds from a pre-rolled sheet of puff pastry

(or roll a block of puff pastry to about 5mm/¼") using a 7cm (2¾") cookie/scone cutter. For one round I could get 15 discs: you will need three per person.

10 Place each disc on a baking sheet lined with baking parchment. Place another sheet of baking parchment over the discs and top with another baking sheet to stop the pastry discs from puffing in the oven.

11 Bake in the oven at 160°C/320°F fan (Gas 4) for 10–15 minutes or until golden.

12 Leave the pastry discs to cool, then pipe out the pastry cream on each layer, interspersing with wild strawberries and finish off with a dusting of icing/confectioner's sugar.

13 Serve within 2 hours, as these are best eaten fresh.

Right and bottom photos show Wallace Fountains, which are found throughout the city, providing free drinking water for passers-by.

Wild Blackberry Millefeuille

MILLEFEUILLE AUX MÛRES SAUVAGES

Nut free

Makes 8
Preparation time: 30 minutes
Chilling time: 1 hour 30 minutes
Cooking time: 30 minutes
Temperature: 160°C/320°F fan (Gas 4)

Spiced blackberry pastry cream:
500g milk
2 cloves, 1 cinnamon stick, 1 star anise
6 egg yolks
50g sugar
40g cornflour (cornstarch)
2 tbsps crème de mûr or cassis (optional)
120g white chocolate, broken into bits
3 x 2g sheets gelatine
50g blackberry purée (or use frozen dark fruits, stewed)
Blackberry or blueberry jam (optional)
2 punnets of fresh wild blackberries (3—4 per pastry)

Pastry:
500g pure-butter puff pastry (or 2 x 250g packets ready-rolled puff pastry)
Icing sugar (confectioner's sugar)

Serve with a spiced Chai tea, a berry good fruit tea or a festive Kir Royal with crème de mûr

As a new arrival in the 7th arrondissement in Paris, I was amazed at the rows of enticing-looking cheap bottles of wine at our local supermarket. The wines, however, were as dry and acidic as the smile-less faces at the cash desk. The classic French kir apéritif was the happiest solution to disguise the sour-tasting wines.

For a festive occasion, the kir's chic big, bubbly sister is the Kir Royal made with Champagne, but traditionally and best served with a Crémant de Bourgogne, dry sparkling wine from Burgundy.

Here I've interspersed this flaky stack of wild blackberries with a white chocolate cream but added a fruit purée to the bottom layer for extra colour.

1 Preheat the oven to 160°C/320°F fan (Gas 4).

2 Soak the gelatine in cold water for 10 minutes. Heat the milk in a saucepan with the spices. Leave to infuse for 10 minutes off the heat then remove the spices. Make the pastry cream according to the method on page 72. At the end of cooking, take off the heat and whisk in the white chocolate then the gelatine (squeezed of excess water) until melted.

3 Transfer half of the cream to a bowl, cover with cling film and cool. With the rest of the cream, whisk in the fruit purée and, if using, mix in the 2 tablespoons of crème de mûr. Cover with cling film, allow to cool, then chill.

4 Roll out the pastry to a 5mm (¼") thickness. Cut out 24 rectangles about 10cm x 5cm (4" x 2"). Place each rectangle on a baking sheet lined with baking parchment. Place another sheet of baking parchment over them and top with another baking sheet to stop the pastry from puffing in the oven. Bake in the oven for 15 minutes. Remove the rectangles and place on a wire rack to cool. Prepare the pastry rectangles as described on pages 132—5.

5 Whisk each of the chilled creams and transfer them to piping bags with a serrated and/or plain tip. If using, spread a thin layer of jam on eight of the non-glossy pastry layers. Pipe the creams out onto the rectangle bases, and decorate with fresh wild blackberries, and press down.

PARISIAN MACARONS
A Pastry with Feet

Paris's ambassador of pastry!

The ultimate bestselling teatime treat in Paris is the *macaron*. It travels worldwide like Paris's Ambassador of Pastry. I emphasise the maca*ron* pronunciation not to sound posh (or to prove that after over 22 years I can get by in French) but so that it's not confused with the very different coconut confection called the maca*roon* (*rocher coco* or *congolais* in French).

In the looks department, the macaron has risen to super-model status since its very modest début in 1533 by Catherine de Medicis, when she brought a similar but rougher looking Italian confection to France.

Using the same ingredients of ground almonds (almond flour), egg whites and sugar it wasn't until the 1900s that Pierre Desfontaines, the second cousin of Louis Ernest Ladurée, came up with the look of the new Parisian macaron (or *Gerbet*) at the family's original pâtisserie in Rue Royale, which started out as a bakery there in 1862. He's credited with having the idea of sandwiching two shells together with chocolate ganache. I'm sure he would have been proud that his descendant is today associated with fashion designers who sometimes develop unique macaron presentation boxes for the famous store!

And so, a rising pâtisserie star was born that is now also seen in the fashionable streets of the USA, Japan, Malaysia, the Middle East and all over the rest of Europe. The macaron even has its own festival: the *fête du macaron*, on March 20, when many pâtisseries (part of the French Relais Desserts group) participate in the charitable event.

Never mind the presentation boxes, but those majestic macaron tower window displays with their pastel shades, glistening gold, vibrant rainbow colours or stylish chocolate creations, have always knocked me off the pavement (about as much as serious women with bigger umbrellas, but that's another story.)

Classic recipes are always to be found – but any flavour is possible with a macaron. Floral *parfums*, spicy inventions, fun "childhood-memory" flavours, or the occasional, daring savoury-sweet concoctions to serve as an *apéritif* – many pâtisseries regularly produce these limited-edition taste experiences.

There's something particularly alluring about *making* Parisian macarons. For a start, they are seen as a challenge to make. It's not like making a cake where you can throw in your butter, sugar, flour and eggs; mix, bake and, hey presto, cake!

It's about precision: **measuring your ingredients by weight rather than volume** and following

A macaron(left) and a macaroon (right)

a few simple but very important rules. If I've lost you here, don't worry: it's so much easier than you think! Before you know it, you may also find yourself jumping up and down in front of the oven, doing the macaron dance when you discover that your macarons have feet!

Feet? Yes, in macaron talk, we *macaronivores* love feet. If it doesn't have a ruffled, frilly foot or *pied*, it's not a macaron.

The most incredible motivation in making these beauties, though, is not just the feet. First and foremost is their taste: crispy, meringue-like on the outside and smooth, fondant flavoured heaven in the inside – which comes from allowing them to mature for at least 24 hours. They will be at their best for up to several days (kept chilled in the

fridge), unlike other bakery items which are best eaten on the day of baking.

The bonus feature is the **wow factor** – they're a perfect trump card for entertaining, especially as they can be frozen in advance.

As in my first book, *Mad About Macarons*, in these recipes I use the French meringue method, rather than the Italian meringue method that requires using a sugar thermometer. Personally, I find the results from French meringue are just as good. Why complicate things if something works?

Please just ensure that you are precise with your ingredients and stick to the recipe!

You have a blank canvas for your macaron flavours. Make your own favourite flavour-combinations based on these ideas. Say it with flowers in the following floral-scented macarons or make classic pairings with a little twist; and, just for fun, create effervescent macarons that literally pop in the mouth!

Don't forget that all the macarons in this chapter are **gluten free**.

Macarons

MACARON SHELLS: A BLANK CANVAS FOR FLAVOUR

Gluten free

Makes approx. 35 macarons (70 shells)
Preparation time: 30 minutes
Resting time: 30 minutes
Cooking time: 12 minutes per tray
Temperature: 160°C/320°F fan (Gas 4)

120g ground almonds (almond flour)
180g icing sugar (confectioner's sugar)
100g egg whites – from approx. 3 eggs
(whites aged for 3–5 days in a closed
jar in the fridge and brought up to room
temperature before baking)
65g caster sugar (superfine sugar)
Colouring of choice (powder or
concentrated paste)

You will need:-
Digital scales
Oven thermometers
Large bowl (flat bottomed if possible)
Large medium/fine sieve
Three baking sheets
Baking parchment/silicone sheets
Electric food mixer
Large flexible spatula
Pâtisserie scraper
40cm (16") piping bag
A plain tip piping nozzle (8–10mm/⅜")
(See Baking Equipment, page 211)

1   Line three flat baking sheets with perfectly flat baking parchment and set aside. (Good quality baking parchment/paper is preferable to a silicone mat when making macarons, as the resulting feet size is far better.) Prepare a 40cm (16") piping bag with an 8–10mm plain tip (⅜").

2   Sift the ground almonds with the icing sugar using a medium sieve. Discard any large, coarse pieces of ground almonds. Mix well to incorporate icing sugar and almonds. (For chocolate macarons, sift in 10g of cocoa at this point.)

3   Whisk the egg whites (at room temperature) to glossy firm peaks, gradually adding the caster sugar. (Ensure the bowl and whisk are perfectly clean. Any trace of fat, yolk or soap will affect the success.)

4   If making coloured macarons, then add colouring towards the end of mixing – a good pinch to ½ teaspoon of powdered colour. Continue to whisk a few seconds more to incorporate the colouring.

5 Incorporate the beaten egg whites into the dry ingredients using a large flexible spatula. Mix well. There is no need to "fold" the mixture, just mix well. The batter will be a bit thick and clumpy at this point.

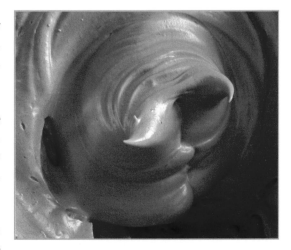

6 Using a plastic scraper (or continuing with the spatula), work to smooth the mixture (macaronnage). Work slowly. Press down well on the sides or bottom of the bowl with the scraper, going back and forward, to press out the air bubbles from the mixture.

7 Lift the spatula regularly and drop the batter. As soon as you have a smooth brilliant mixture that drops like a "ribbon" from the spatula or scraper, stop!

8 See the pictures, right, showing meringue with stiff peaks, the incorporation of meringue and almonds, and finally, the mixture as it should look when it has been sufficiently mixed. Too much mixing results in flat macarons with cracked tops; and under-mixing will result in dull, bumpy shells.

RUNNY BATTER

Runny or overmixed batter will result in cracked, uneven, over-moist macarons. Poor quality eggs can result in runny batter. Also ensure that your whites aren't too old. They should be aged in an airtight jar for 3–5 days, no more. Whisk up your egg whites stiffly too.

You could still save an overmixed mixture. Leave your macaron shells to air a lot longer than the normal 30 mins. I'd suggest 1½ hours or until they have a distinct hard shell.

Turn down the top of the bag before putting the mixture in it (that way you can unfold the bag when the mixture is in it and you won't have a mess at the top, or on your work surface).

Twist the end of the bag where the nozzle is to stop the mixture running out while you spoon it into the bag. (Untwist when you want to pipe, obviously!)

Secure the top of the bag by twisting or using a clip.

Keep a secure hold of each end of the bag. Control is the key to good piping.

Remember that gravity will play a part! Press the tip right down on the baking sheet. Squeeze lightly and finish off with a flourish.

9 Transfer the batter to a 40cm (16″) piping bag with a plain tip (8–10mm/⅜″). Spoon in the mixture using the spatula.

10 Pipe out 3cm-diameter (1¼″) rounds. Press the tip right down on the paper then finish off with a flourish to obtain a nice round. Leave a good space between each as they spread out.

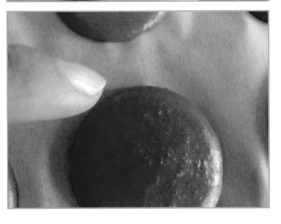

11 Leave for about 30 minutes to air. This helps produce their feet. At this point you can sprinkle with poppy seeds, chopped nuts, etc. They are ready to bake when they are hard to the touch. If not, air for slightly longer. (This is the time to make your filling.)

...eat the oven to 160°C/320°F fan (Gas 3). This is where you will need to experiment and get to know your oven well. It may need a 150–155°C/300°F fan (Gas 2) setting (or slightly higher if you don't have a fan-assisted oven). I cook one shelf of macarons at a time in the middle of the oven but you may need to place them a shelf higher.

13 Bake for 10–12 minutes. After 3 minutes, you will see the feet forming (this is when we do a wee dance in front of the oven). After 8 minutes, do the "wobble" test: touch the top of a macaron and gently move your finger side to side. Depending on how much it moves, cook for 2–4 minutes longer until firm. Chocolate macarons will need another couple of minutes.

14 When ready, leave on the baking tray until completely cool. Remove them all carefully. Marry up the shells in pairs according to size, one row flat side up and one row flat side down.

15 Prepare the piping bag with your chosen filling and pipe onto each upturned shell. Place its partner on top, using a circular motion to squash the shell down on the filling.

16 Transfer the macarons to a pastry box or airtight container and store in the fridge for 24 hours for the filling to do its magic.

CRACKS AND HOLLOWS

Your oven can be the biggest culprit for cracks, hollows and uneven baking of macarons. Is your oven doing what it's saying it is? Use an oven thermometer and, if necessary, adjust the temperature.

Rose and Orange-Blossom Macarons

MACARONS À LA ROSE ET FLEUR D'ORANGER

Gluten free

Makes approx. 35 macarons (70 shells)
Preparation time: 30 minutes
Resting time: 30 minutes
Cooking time: 12 minutes
Temperature: 160°C/320°F fan (Gas 4)

Shells:

120g ground almonds (almond flour)
180g icing sugar (confectioner's sugar)
100g egg whites
65g caster sugar (superfine sugar)
Pinch of pink powder or paste colouring

Filling:

75g single cream
1 tbsp rosewater (see page 30)
1 tbsp orange-blossom water
1 egg yolk
15g caster sugar (superfine sugar)
10g cornflour (cornstarch)
80g unsalted organic butter, softened

Pair with an off-dry pink Champagne

For Valentine's Day, Parisian boutiques often say it with rose macarons but, as I also love orange-blossom macarons, I couldn't make up my mind. So I combined the two and produced a rose *and* orange-blossom macaron. It's bliss. You can taste both flavours in there.

Returning to the birthplace of the Parisian macaron in the 1900s, it was in **Rue Royale** that Louis Ernest Ladurée opened his original bakery in 1862. After Baron Haussmann's facelift of Paris in 1871, Louis's wife (a wealthy hotelier's daughter from Rouen) had the idea of enlarging the shop into a tearoom. The ladies loved an opportunity to come out of the house for afternoon teatime, especially as it probably gave them an excuse to exhibit yet another change of clothes! I tried that one on my husband but somehow he didn't take it seriously.

Who needs a bouquet of flowers on Valentine's Day when you can be seduced by these light delights – when paired with an off-dry pink Champagne your toes will curl. The best lovers say it with homemade macarons. Just saying.

1 Make the basic macaron recipe, pages 146–50, adding pink colouring.
2 To make the filling, heat the cream with the rose and orange blossom waters in a saucepan.

3 Whisk together the yolk and sugar until frothy. Whisk in the cornflour until smooth. Add the hot floral cream to the mix then transfer back to the pan and continue to whisk over a medium heat until the mixture thickens.

4 Remove from the heat and cover with cling film (plastic wrap). Leave to cool completely, till room temperature.

5 Cream the room temperature butter until pale then briskly whisk in the room temperature cream mixture until smooth. *(Don't cut corners. I've tried that! If you just whisk cold butter into warm cream the mixture could curdle.)*

6 Pipe filling on one of each macaron pair of shells, and assemble. Leave the filling to penetrate into the shells for 24 hours in a pastry box in the fridge.

FLORAL FLAVOURS

To make elderflower macarons, replace the orange-blossom and rosewater with 3 tablespoons elderflower syrup (I use Monin's).

How to make Valentine Macaron Hearts

To pipe out Valentine hearts, make a distinct "V" shape with two separate strokes of the piping bag as in the diagram. As you're piping them out, press out using more pressure at the top of each line. They will quickly spread out to form a heart. Leave to air before baking as usual.

How to Make a Macaron Cone Centrepiece

This is a centrepiece with the wow-factor for special teatime occasions. Maybe for Christmas or Hallowe'en parties, for example. Use a polystyrene cone. Wrap some crêpe paper around it, sticking it in place with cocktail sticks. They not only keep the paper in place but by sticking them in two-thirds of the way into the polystyrene, you can pierce each macaron in place.

For Christmas, use dark green crêpe paper for a Christmas tree effect or, for Hallowe'en, stick on a clean witch's hat (or black paper) then poke through the cocktail sticks.

For Stockists, see page 219.

Lemon and Grapefruit Macarons

MACARONS AU CITRON ET PAMPLEMOUSSE

Gluten free

Makes approx. 35 macarons (70 shells)
Preparation time: 30 minutes
Resting time: 30 minutes
Cooking time: 12 minutes
Temperature: 160°C/320°F fan (Gas 4)

Shells:

120g ground almonds (almond flour)
180g icing sugar (confectioner's sugar)
100g egg whites
65g caster sugar (superfine sugar)
Good pinch of yellow powder or paste
food colouring

Filling:

80g pink grapefruit juice (from approx.
1 grapefruit)
Zest of an unwaxed lemon
50g sugar
1 egg
2 egg yolks
70g butter, cold and diced

Serve with Darjeeling or Earl Grey teas

I picked the wrong end of the longest street in Paris, **Rue Vaugirard**. It's 4.3km, to be precise, and it was during a heatwave. When I found Pierre Hermé's pâtisserie it had a queue well outside the door. This was years ago when I had no idea what to choose and how much it would cost. When it was finally my turn to be served, I panicked, hastily picking eight macarons, of which most were refreshing lemon, and ran out the door. I planned to share them with the family at home but, judging by the heat, it wasn't the best plan. (You'll know what I mean if you spend a fortune on macarons and discover them later in the bag as a mushed mosaic!) I ate them all by the time I found the metro. These days I would have simply headed to the more central but hidden street of **Rue Cambon**, and enjoy tasting them in the Tuileries Gardens across the road.

1 Follow the basic macaron recipe, pages 146–50, and add yellow colouring.

2 For the filling, put the grapefruit juice, zest, egg, egg yolks and sugar in a saucepan and, over a low–medium heat, whisk until the mixture foams then gradually thickens. Take off the heat (and sieve the mixture to remove the zest – or skip if you don't mind that texture). Add the cold butter, whisking until smooth.

3 When cool, leave to chill and thicken in the fridge for an hour.

4 Pipe filling on one of each macaron pair of shells, and assemble. Refrigerate for 24 hours.

VARIATIONS

Try with all kinds of citrus fruits: lemon, lime, orange or blood orange.

RUE
DE BOURBON
LE CHÂTEAU

Salted Caramel Macarons

MACARONS AU CARAMEL BEURRE SALÉ

Gluten free

Makes approx. 35 macarons (70 shells)
Preparation time: 30 minutes
Resting time: 30 minutes
Cooking time: 12 minutes
Temperature: 160°C/320°F fan (Gas 4)

Shells:
120g ground almonds (almond flour)
180g icing sugar (confectioner's sugar)
100g egg whites
65g caster sugar (superfine sugar)
Good pinch caramel (brown/yellow)
powder or paste food colouring

Salted caramel cream:
1 x 2g sheet gelatine
100g sugar
100g cream, warmed
60g butter
½ tsp sea salt (or *fleur de sel*)
150g mascarpone

Serve with English breakfast or green tea

LUSTRE DUST
Add the shiny, festive look to your macarons by brushing on (or rubbing with your finger) bronze, silver or gold lustre dust (found online or in the food colouring section of specialist stores).

Why is it that salt added to caramel is so agonisingly addictive? Salted caramel is surprisingly recent: *caramel au beurre salé* (CBS) was invented in the 1970s by Henri Le Roux in Quiberon, where salted butter is added to most Brittany specialities. Now, thankfully we can taste the genuine thing in his chocolate shop or *caramélier* in **Rue de Bourbon le Château** in Paris.

You'll see many salted caramel pastry offerings in Paris using *fleur de sel*. Literally "flower of salt", it's the most expensive salt since it's hand-harvested by scraping only the top thin layer of white salt crystals before it sinks to the bottom of large salt pans. It's most famously collected in the town of Guérande, off the coast of Brittany. Fleur de sel is known to dissolve quicker than normal salt and so it has more flavour when added at the end of cooking.

1 Follow the basic macaron recipe, pages 146–50, and add caramel colouring.

2 Soak the gelatine in cold water for 10 minutes.

3 Heat the sugar in a small saucepan until a golden, syrupy caramel forms. This should take about 10 minutes. Meanwhile heat the cream in a separate pan or in the microwave. Turn down the heat and add the warmed cream gradually (ensure it's warm, otherwise you'll have the boiling caramel spitting at you!).

4 Take off the heat and melt in the butter, stirring with a wooden spoon.

5 Add the gelatine. Leave to cool on the counter for 15 minutes.

6 Add the salt and gradually whisk in the mascarpone vigorously until you have a smooth texture.

7 Chill in the fridge for at least 30 minutes.

8 Transfer the caramel cream to a piping bag, pipe on the filling to each macaron couple, topping off with the other macaron shell to assemble.

Chocolate, Honey & Orange Blossom Macarons

MACARONS AU CHOCOLAT, MIEL ET FLEUR D'ORANGER

Gluten free

Makes approx. 35 macarons (70 shells)
Preparation time: 30 minutes
Resting time: 30 minutes
Cooking time: 12 minutes
Temperature: 160°C/320°F fan (Gas 4)

Shells:
120g ground almonds (almond flour)
180g icing sugar (confectioner's sugar)
100g egg whites
65g caster sugar (superfine sugar)
Good pinch orange (red/yellow) powdered food colouring

Filling:
150g dark cooking chocolate (72% cacao solids)
150g whipping cream
1 tbsp honey
1 tbsp orange blossom water
40g unsalted organic butter

Serve with Assam or Oolong tea

These "healthy" macarons are inspired by the oldest *chocolaterie* in Paris, just a block away from the church of Saint Germain des Prés. Opened by Sulpice Debauve in 1800 after the French Revolution, he was quite a businessman with 65 depots and a mail-order system set up within just a few years. Previously pharmacist to King Louis XVI and Queen Marie-Antoinette at Versailles, Monsieur Debauve's aim was to provide healthy chocolates to cure whatever ailed his royal "patients". Costly sought-after chocolate labelled as medicine was a crafty way around paying taxes at the time, as everything was taxable except medical expenses.

As Queen Marie Antoinette was rather partial to her chocolate doses in the form of *pistoles* – wafer thin disks – she most probably enjoyed Monsieur Debauve's *chocolat des dames*, as orange blossom water was added to act as an anti-spasmodic treatment for ladies' monthly ailments. Other most likely natural pick-me-up remedies like honey, ginger, almond and coffee were also added. Debauve died at the fine age of 79, so there must be something healthy in eating good dark chocolate!

I'm no pharmacist but I recommend you take at least one of these healthy macarons a day (keep a stock in the freezer and defrost 30 minutes before eating at room temperature) with a cup of Assam tea infused for 5 minutes, served with a cloud of milk.

DARK CHOCOLATE IS GOOD FOR YOU
It's a better antioxidant than milk chocolate, blueberries and red wine. It's full of magnesium and so helps fight fatigue and depression. A little a day keeps the doctor and the blues away! The higher the percentage of cacao the better, and usually there's less sugar in dark chocolate.

1 Follow the basic macaron recipe, pages 146–50, and add the orange colouring.

2 To make the ganache, break up the chocolate into pieces in a bowl. In a saucepan, bring the cream, honey and orange blossom water to near boiling point then pour over the broken chocolate.

3 Stir constantly in the middle with a wooden spoon until smooth. Add the butter to give the ganache a healthy, glossy coat.

4 Leave to cool but be careful not to wait too long as the chocolate hardens quite quickly. Transfer to a piping bag, arrange the macaron shells in pairs, pipe filling onto one shell of each pair and assemble the macarons.

5 Leave in the fridge for at least 24 hours, preferably 36, before serving at room temperature.

VARIATIONS

If you prefer plain chocolate macarons without the orange blossom, use 150g dark chocolate and 150g whipping cream. If you prefer milk chocolate macarons, use 150g milk chocolate and only 120g cream. Replace the orange blossom water with your favourite espresso coffee.

MACARONS AT THEIR BEST

To enjoy macarons at their best, keep them chilled for at least 24 hours then take them out of the fridge 30 minutes before serving (chocolate macarons are even better after 36 hours).

Fizzy Orange Macarons

Gluten free

Makes approx. 35 macarons (70 shells)
Preparation time: 30 minutes
Resting time: 30 minutes
Cooking time: 12 minutes
Temperature: 160°C/320°F fan (Gas 4)

Shells:

120g ground almonds (almond flour)
180g icing sugar (confectioner's sugar)
100g egg whites
65g caster sugar (superfine sugar)
Good pinch orange (red/yellow) powdered
Food colouring
Orange edible glitter sprinkles (optional)
2 tbsps popping candy (*sucre pétillant*)

Filling:

100g Orangina ™ or another fizzy orange drink
100g orange-flavour, sugar-frosted gelatine sweets
55g white chocolate
1 heaped tbsp mascarpone

Serve with Orangina ™

For serious macaron lovers, I recommend a detour off the tourist track to Acide Macaron, a favourite macaron and pastry boutique of many Parisians. It is now expanded into a tea salon in **Rue des Moines**, although the pastry chef prefers to refer to it as a "dessert restaurant". If you don't have much time in Paris, however, the good news is that another boutique (without the tearoom) is also in **Rue du Bac**.

Just across the road from Rue des Moines is the floral **Square des Batignolles**, an ideal tasting spot next to the little lake.

Not long ago, I discovered *sucre pétillant* (popping candy) in a few épiceries in Paris (now they're in the baking section in many Paris supermarkets) and so the idea of creating a fizzy-drink macaron with this fun sugar was too tempting.

To taste them at their best, lick off the popping candy first, then pop the macaron in for a fun, fizzy explosion.

1 Following the basic recipe, pages 146–50, make the macaron shells using a pinch of orange colouring (red/yellow). Just after piping out the rounds, gently draw a line from the middle to the top of each with a cocktail stick to produce a pointed tip. Just before baking, sprinkle with the orange glitter.

2 To make the filling, melt the sweets, fizzy orange and white chocolate in a small saucepan over a gentle heat. As soon as it has melted, whisk in the mascarpone and set aside to cool. The gelatine in the sweets will thicken it up quite quickly as it cools, so it will be manageable to pipe it onto the shells. If it hardens up too quickly, reheat it gently for a few seconds over a low heat

3 Sprinkle *sucre pétillant* (popping candy) on your macarons just before serving.

VARIATIONS

You can replace the Orangina™ with Fanta™. Also, using cola and cola-sweets, you could make cola macarons (pictured far left). Just add some black colouring to the filling, and create a fizzy effect by flicking the macaron shells with a small paintbrush dipped in black food colouring, just before they go in the oven.

RUE
RAMBUTEAU
(1781 - 1869)
PRÉFET DE LA SEINE
DE 1833 A 1848

1er Arrṭ

Raspberry, Lime and Tarragon "Maclairs"

MACARONS À LA FRAMBOISE, CITRON VERT ET L'ESTRAGON – FAÇON ÉCLAIR

Gluten free

Makes approx. 15 macarons (30 shells)
Preparation time: 30 minutes
Resting time: 30 minutes
Cooking time: 12 minutes
Temperature: 160°C/320°F fan (Gas 4)

Shells:
120g ground almonds (almond flour)
180g icing sugar (confectioner's sugar)
100g egg whites
65g caster sugar (superfine sugar)
¼ tsp of raspberry/framboise pink
powdered colouring
1 tsp dried raspberry powder (optional)

Filling:
200g fresh (or frozen) raspberries
1 tbsp fresh tarragon, finely chopped
2 tbsps lime juice
180g white chocolate, broken into bits

Serve with Ceylon or Yunnan teas

Starting from **Châtelet Les Halles**, head along **Rue Rambuteau** for just a few blocks and you're already in the 3rd arrondissement, staring in the pâtisserie windows of the likes of Les Fées Pâtissières and Pain du Sucre.

What I love about the high-end pastry shops is how they marry up unsuspecting combinations, like this one which I discovered via a tartlet and transformed it into a macaron, or rather "maclair".

Ensure you pick a good quality white chocolate that doesn't contain fats other than cocoa butter.

1 Following the basic macaron recipe, pages 146–50, and make the macaron shells adding the pink colouring and raspberry powder (if using).

2 To make your "*maclairs*", pipe your macaron shells as described in the basic recipe but in elongated, longer strips of about 8–10cm (3–4") like an éclair.

3 Blitz the raspberries in a food processor for about 3–4 minutes, until the seeds are well and truly crushed. (If you really don't like seeds, you can filter out seeds using a sieve at this point.)

4 Gently heat the raspberry purée in a saucepan with the lime juice and tarragon – over a low-medium heat – and gradually stir in the white chocolate bits. Stir with a wooden spoon, until the white chocolate has completely melted and blended with the fruit.

5 Set aside to cool then refrigerate for an hour before piping out the filling onto your maclair shells.

VARIATION

To make larger Valentine's macarons, pipe out 6 macaron hearts and 6 slightly larger macaron shells (about 5cm). Pipe out ½ portion of vanilla pastry cream (page 72) mixed with 3 tablespoons of mascarpone and garnish with your favourite berries.

Rhubarb and Poppy Macarons

MACARONS À LA RHUBARBE ET COQUELICOT

Gluten free

Makes approx. 35 macarons (70 shells)
Preparation time: 30 minutes
Resting time: 30 minutes
Cooking time: 12 minutes
Temperature: 160°C/320°F fan (Gas 4)

120g ground almonds (almond flour)
180g icing sugar (confectioner's sugar)
100g egg whites
65g caster sugar (superfine sugar)
Good pinch red powdered food colouring
1 tbsp poppy seeds

Filling:

90g single cream
5 tbsps rhubarb compote
1 egg yolk
15g caster sugar
15g cornflour (cornstarch)
75g unsalted organic butter, softened
½ tsp natural poppy aroma (*arôme coquelicot*, see Stockists, page 219).
If poppy flavouring is hard to find then why not combine rhubarb with vanilla, ginger, almond or orange flavours

Serve with Darjeeling tea or pink lemonade

If you have more time to spend in Paris, head to the 16th arrondissement where the **Marmottan Museum** is home to many famous Impressionist paintings and treasures – including Monet's pipe. In mid May, when the poppies spring out to announce summer, take a day trip to his gardens in **Giverny**. Pack a few poppy macarons in a cooler bag for a civilised picnic and enjoy them in a shady spot along by the **River Seine**, where Monet loved to paint out in the open, particularly on his floating rowing boat workshop.

The French love adding poppy aroma to macarons, as it perhaps reminds them of bright red *coquelicot* sweets from childhood. Many pâtisseries marry sweet poppy with strawberry (my favourite are from Mulot's in **Rue du Pas-de-la-Mule** – the other one is in **Rue de Seine**) but the rhubarb just adds that slight acidity.

1 Follow the basic macaron recipe, adding a pinch of red powdered colouring. Once the shells have aired, sprinkle on the poppy seeds before baking.

2 To make the cream filling, heat the cream in a saucepan until almost boiling.

3 In a bowl, whisk the egg yolk and sugar until white and creamy and mix in the cornflour and rhubarb compote. Pour the warmed cream onto the yolk mixture.

4 Transfer back to the pan and the heat, whisking briskly until the cream thickens, then take off the heat and cool in the fridge for 10 minutes.

5 Cream the butter with a wooden spoon until it is pale.

6 When the mixture is cool, add the poppy aroma and beat in the softened, creamed butter. Transfer to a piping bag, arrange the macaron shells in pairs, pipe filling onto one shell of each pair and assemble.

7 Leave in the fridge for at least 24 hours before serving.

RUE
DU PAS
DE LA MULE

4e Arr^t

Giant Paris-Brest Macarons

MACARONS GÉANTS FAÇON PARIS-BREST

Gluten free

Makes approx. 20 macarons (40 shells)
Preparation time: 45 minutes
Resting time: 30 minutes
Cooking time: 12 minutes
Temperature: 160°C/320°F fan (Gas 4)

80g ground almonds (almond flour)
40g ground hazelnuts
180g icing sugar (confectioner's sugar)
100g egg whites
65g caster sugar (superfine sugar)
¼ tsp powdered caramel (brown/yellow)
colouring

Hazelnut praline:
80g whole hazelnuts
60g sugar

Praline buttercream filling:
250ml milk
1 tbsp instant/soluble coffee
2 egg yolks
40g caster sugar
1 tsp vanilla extract
20g cornflour (cornstarch)
Praline, crushed (as above)
100g butter, softened

Serve with Assam or rooibos teas

The Paris-Brest pastry's traditional crown shape was inspired by a bicycle wheel. Invented in 1910 by Louis Durand, a pastry chef in **Maisons-Laffitte**, he wanted to celebrate the Paris-Brest-Paris cycle race that passed through his Paris suburb in **Avenue Longeuil**. It didn't take much research to find that one out since we lived around the corner from his shop for five years. We had plenty of opportunities to taste his famous choux pastry creation, now copied the world over. Having tasted them on a regular basis, just for experimental purposes, I think one of their little secret ingredients of the toasted praline buttercream filling is coffee and, most importantly, home-made praline.

I felt pretty nutty the day my flapping arms just about knocked a cyclist off the road. Chatting to a French neighbour on the street, I was totally unaware that my hand, arm and shoulder gestures had gradually become just as Frenchily expressive as hers, as arms waved passionately about in tempo with our discussion. So if you hire a *Vélib'* bicycle in Paris, be aware of scintillating, arm-flapping discussions *à la française* at the side of the road, especially in such narrow streets like **Rue des Saints Pères (towards Boulevard Saint Germain)**.

This is a gluten free, lighter version for teatime of the classic Paris-Brest dessert, replacing its characteristic choux wheel with individual giant macarons. The taste is transformed by making your own homemade praline, using good quality hazelnuts (I buy mine in a health food store). Try to avoid ready-made packs of praline in the supermarket baking section: it's not at all the same thing! I often make double quantities of praline and store it in a jam jar for sprinkling on more treats later.

For a more classic Paris-Brest, turn to page 187.

1 Dry fry the hazelnuts, without any oil, in a frying pan over a medium heat for 5 minutes.

2 In a small saucepan, heat the sugar over a medium heat with a couple of drops of water until the caramel turns a dark golden colour (no more than

5 minutes – keep your eye on it as you don't want the caramel to burn). Quickly tip the toasted hazelnuts in the caramel, stir until they are fully coated and briskly pour out the hot, sticky mixture directly onto a slightly oiled or non-stick baking tray. Leave to cool, fill the saucepan with water and leave in the sink (this will make your washing up so much easier!)

3   When cool, break up the caramel and pound it to a powder using a mortar and pestle or much easier, using a food processor.

4   Gently boil the milk in a medium-sized saucepan with the coffee.

5   Whisk the yolks, vanilla extract and sugar in a bowl until light and creamy. Add the cornflour and continue to whisk until a smooth paste.

6   Pour half of the boiling milk over the yolk mix then return the rest of the mix to the saucepan, whisking constantly over a medium heat until the mixture thickens (about 5 minutes). Take off the heat and immediately cover with cling film to avoid a skin forming on the cream. After about 10 minutes, transfer to the fridge and chill for about an hour.

7   In a large bowl, cream the butter until light and fluffy. Whisk in the cooled cream and add the hazelnut praline.

8   Leave to cool in the fridge for 10–15 minutes. Pipe out the filling using a tip that's at least 12mm (½"), so that no nut bits clog up the tip, and garnish half of the macaron shells. Assemble the remaining macarons.

PRALINE

Make double quantities of the praline and store the other half in a sealed jar: it's so handy for sprinkling on pastries, macarons, desserts and crumbles – or making a Paris-Brest-Edinburgh.

Mojito Cocktail Macarons
FOR GOÛTER OR HAPPY HOUR!

Gluten free

Makes approx. 35 macarons (70 shells)
Preparation time: 30 minutes
Resting time: 30 minutes
Cooking time: 12 minutes
Temperature: 160°C/320°F fan (Gas 4)

Shells:
100g egg whites
65g caster sugar (superfine sugar)
80g ground almonds (almond flour)
40g ground hazelnuts
160g icing sugar
¼ tsp powdered green colouring

Ganache filling:
130g white chocolate
50g whipping cream
Juice of half a lime
Zest of an unwaxed lime
10 mint leaves, very finely chopped
20g dark rum (or white rum)

Serve with mint tea, sparkling water with lime or wait until Happy Hour

Where were these revitalising cocktail macarons when I needed them? Three weeks after arriving in 1993, I felt ready to tackle a self-improvement exercise at the *Grands Magasins'* sales: *les Soldes*. Finding my first bargain jumper of joy winking from beneath a classic Mont-Blanc of own-store labels, it was instantly snatched out of my weak, pathetic fingers. Who was I to retaliate? You see, the Parisians perceived I was no local: last season's bright green golf sweaters gave me away as much as the 80s big hair, fixed like a helmet. Using French hairspray was surely enough to blend in; or so I thought.

My new French friends and colleagues politely empathised but it was clear: something of a fashion revolution was needed to calm it all down. Everything had to cling more to *ze body*, hairdo included.

Since then, you are much more likely to find me sneaking into the store's gourmet section via **Rue de Provence**, since many macaron and pastry houses are under the same roof, including Sadaharu Aoki. What a relief. Is it a sign of a *lazy gourmet* to feel fashionably at home sweet home here instead?

If you feel like merging 4 o'clock teatime into 5 o'clock Happy Hour, these gluten-free treats are just like the real thing in a cocktail glass – and best reserved for the adults!

1 Break up the white chocolate into bits and melt in a bowl over a pan of simmering water (bain-marie.) As soon as the chocolate has melted, take off the heat.

2 Briskly whisk in the cream, lime zest and juice, mint and rum and set aside to cool in the fridge for at least an hour.

3 Follow the basic recipe for macarons and add the green colouring – make it quite intensely green.

4 When manageable, transfer the filling to a piping back and pipe onto each macaron half and assemble.

5 Store in the fridge for 24 hours before serving.

9me. ARR^t.
RUE
DE PROVENCE

1er Arrᵗ

**RUE
SAINT-HONORÉ**

Chocolate, Cinnamon and Chestnut Macarons

MACARONS CHOCOLAT, CANNELLE ET CRÈME DE MARRON

Gluten free

Makes approx. 35 macarons (70 shells)
Preparation time: 30 minutes
Resting time: 30 minutes
Cooking time: 12 minutes
Temperature: 160°C (320°F, Gas 4)

Shells:
100g egg whites
65g caster sugar (superfine sugar)
80g ground almonds (almond flour)
40g ground hazelnuts
160g icing sugar
10g unsweetened cocoa powder
1 tsp ground cinnamon
A good pinch dark brown powdered food
colouring and pinch of red (optional)

Filling:
125g dark cooking chocolate (at least
64% cacao solids)
125g whipping cream
1 cinnamon stick
100g sweet chestnut purée (*crème de
marron*, Clément Faugier)
1 tsp cinnamon powder
A pinch of sea salt (or *fleur de sel*)
20g unsalted organic butter, softened

Serve with a spiced chai tea

Who makes the best chocolate macaron in Paris? This is a question I'm often asked. It's tough with so many incredible stops to choose from and opinions swing all the time. However, just between you and me, one of my favourite chocolate makers is Pierre Marcolini, who makes his own chocolate from bean to bar. Sourcing different cacao beans from the plantations 20° North or South of the Equator, he blends cacao like a winemaker would. I strongly recommend a tasting in his boutique on **Rue Saint Honoré**, to appreciate artisanal chocolate. His "own blend" chocolate macaron is a luxurious mix of cacao from Venezuela, Cuba and Ghana. With this recipe it feels like festive season at any time of year with the hint of cinnamon and candied chestnut.

1 Follow the basic macaron recipe, pages 146–50, adding the cocoa powder, cinnamon and colouring (although this is optional – adding the red adds a deeper intensity).

2 To make the ganache, break the chocolate into pieces in a bowl. In a saucepan, bring the cream to near boiling point with the cinnamon stick.

3 Take off the heat and cover, leaving the cinnamon to infuse for 10 minutes. Remove the stick, reheat the cream then pour half over the broken chocolate.

4 Stir constantly in the middle with a wooden spoon until it starts to melt and then add the rest of the hot cream till smooth.

5 Mix in the softened butter to make the ganache glossy and when completely melted, mix in the cinnamon powder, salt and chestnut purée.

6 Leave to cool in the fridge for about 10 minutes. Be careful not to wait too long as the chocolate hardens quite quickly (but the chestnut keeps it moist). Transfer to a piping bag, arrange the macaron shells in pairs, pipe filling onto one shell of each pair and assemble the macarons.

7 Leave in the fridge for at least 24 hours, preferably 36, before serving at room temperature.

A FRENCH TEA PARTY
La crème de la crème

The most important ingredient is fun!

Once you have tasted the classic recipes, you'll probably discover that you don't want to stop there. Try out your own flavour and texture combinations and add your own personal twist. Here are just a few fun ideas with a *tour de force* of mixing and matching from the previous chapters to get the pastry rolling and your personalised creations flowing.

The recipes in this chapter are for those special occasions when you feel like being spoiled, so they are longer but, as you break up the different elements, many of the recipe parts can be made in advance and besides, I've cut some corners for you. From the previous recipes, ideally you will have macarons to hand in the fridge or freezer and choux dough still in its piping bag in the fridge. Now it's just a question of organisation.

Don't forget that these recipes aren't demanding complete perfection. The most important ingredient is fun and, above all, enjoying their ultimate taste.

Picture opposite: A "not-so-religieuse" – a choux puff base with dark chocolate glaze, dotted with coffee cream, topped with half a macaron, chocolate ganache and a crumble-topped choux puff.

Chocolate-Earl Grey Tartlets with Orange-Liqueur Crumble Puffs

TARTELETTES CHOCOLAT ET THÉ À LA BERGAMOTE

Makes 4 tartlets
Preparation time: 1 hour
Cooking time: 45 minutes
Chilling time: 2 hours
Temperature 160°C/320°F fan (Gas 4)

Sweet pastry:

65g butter, at room temperature

35g icing sugar (confectioner's sugar)

¼ tsp salt

½ egg

½ tsp vanilla extract

120g plain flour (all-purpose), sifted

Chocolate-earl grey ganache:

160g dark cooking chocolate

80g milk chocolate

240g cream

2 Earl Grey teabags

Choux dough:

35g water

25g milk

¼ tsp sea salt (or *fleur de sel*)

1 tsp sugar

25g butter

35g flour (plain, all-purpose)

1 eggs

Grand Marnier™ pastry cream:

250g full-cream milk

1 vanilla pod

3 egg yolks

40g caster sugar (superfine sugar)

25g cornflour (cornstarch)

2 tbsps Grand Marnier™

Serve with Earl Grey tea

So many tea salons and chocolate shops in Paris serve cakes, pastries and chocolates that have been flavoured with speciality teas or herbal infusions. It's so *tendance* (trendy), darlings. For the ultimate tea-in-cake salon, head to **Rue des Grands Augustins** or the **Carrousel du Louvre**. Founded in 1854, *Mariage Frères* was the first tea shop in Paris and now they also have a tea museum there. Tea came to Europe via Holland then to France in 1636 (and England 14 years later). During the 17th–18th centuries, although popular, it was considered a luxury item.

Louis XIV was reputed to have been a lover of tea as much as of mistresses. Madame de Sévigné, famous for her letters chronicling life in the royal court at the time, mentioned that it was the Marquise de la Sablière who initiated the Chinese fashion of adding milk to tea, a touch that the British later adopted. Personally I don't see this fashion continuing much in Paris these days. I often have to remind servers several times to bring my tiny jug of milk and, *Mon Dieu*, some tea salons even charge you for it!

If you happen to have a little extra choux dough left, then make this your *crème de la crème* teatime tartlet. I suppose you could say the cream puffs have been "choux-laced"! A whisper of Grand Marnier™ brings out the orangey bergamot Earl Grey tea, but for busy gourmets you can leave the choux empty as chouquettes (page 76) and dribble a little melted chocolate over the top.

1 With a half portion of the sweet pastry recipe on pages 106–9, make the plain or chocolate tartlets following the basic recipe (why not make the whole portion and freeze half of the dough). Bake at 160°C/320°F fan (Gas 4) for 12–15 minutes.

2 To make the ganache filling: Break up the chocolate into chunks in a bowl. Heat the cream with the earl grey teabags in a saucepan until nearly boiling. Take off the heat, cover and leave to infuse for 10 minutes. Remove the teabags and reheat the cream to nearly boiling. Pour half of the hot cream directly onto the chocolate.

6e Arrt

RUE
DES GRANDS
AUGUSTINS

3 Stir gently using a wooden spoon, add the rest of the hot cream and combine until the ganache is smooth and silky.

4 When the pastry is cool, pour in the chocolate ganache and leave to cool in the fridge for about an hour.

5 Make choux pastry following instructions on page 64 (except you are making a quarter quantity) or preferably use a quarter quantity of choux pastry that you have previously prepared, and pipe out about 12 choux puffs. Bake and set aside to cool.

6 Make the pastry cream following basic instructions on page 72 and set aside to chill for an hour, covered in cling film. When cold, whisk and add a teaspoon more of Grand Marnier™ to taste, if necessary. Put the cream into a piping bag with a 6–7mm (¼") tip. Pierce a hole at the bottom of each choux puff and pipe in the cream.

7 Garnish each tartlet with three choux puffs. Set aside in the fridge.

8 Remove the tartlets from the fridge 20 minutes before serving, to bring out the flavours.

Café (ou Thé) Gourmand

WHEN LESS IS MORE

In many Parisian *salons de thé*, a popular teatime treat is an espresso coffee served alongside a plate of three mini sweet treats. This is ideal when the menu choice presents too many decadent choices and so this sampler tasting-opportunity is a fun gourmet solution.

Many of them arrive with a small macaron, so why not invent your own *café gourmand* based on the recipes in this book and make yours a decadent threesome with your coffee?

The **Cour du Commerce Saint André**, just off **Boulevard Saint Germain**, is a cobbled passageway that dates back to 1735 and whispers of revolutionaries past. It still has a part of the original glass roof to protect the ladies' dresses of *l'époque* and boasts the oldest café in Paris, Le Procope, where regulars included Voltaire, Benjamin Franklin, George Sand and plotting revolutionaries such as Robespierre, Danton and Marat. Napoleon also left his hat there since he never settled the bill.

The newest addition is Un Dimanche à Paris, an all-chocolate pâtisserie and tea salon, where the hot chocolate and pastries are just as good as the café gourmand. Oh, choices!

What about a cream puff filled with light coffee cream, a chocolate cinnamon macaron and a mini chocolate tigré? What's yours?

Paris-Brest-Edinburgh Choux-Nut

LE PARIS-BREST-EDIMBOURG

Makes 6
Preparation time: 1 hour
Cooking time: 1 hour
Chilling time: 1 hour 30 minutes
Temperature: 160°C/320°F fan (Gas 4)

Choux dough:

75g water
50g milk
1 tsp sea salt (or *fleur de sel*)
1 tbsp sugar
45g butter
75g flour (plain, all-purpose)
2 eggs

Hazelnut praline:

80g whole hazelnuts
60g sugar

Praline buttercream filling:

250g milk
2 tsps instant/soluble coffee
3 egg yolks
40g caster sugar (superfine sugar)
15g cornflour (cornstarch)
Praline, crushed (as above)
50g unsalted butter, softened

Chocolate-whisky ganache

80g dark chocolate (70%)
90g whipping cream
2 tbsps malt whisky (light, not too peaty)

Serve with English breakfast or Yunnan teas

You'll love the Paris-Brest at the Pâtisserie des Rêves in **Rue du Bac** and they have a tea salon in **Rue de Longchamp**. But, cycling on from my Paris-Brest macaron, it's time to add another personal twist to this classic.

Not forgetting my Edinburgh roots, I'm making this pastry jump on the EuroStar and cycle up to Edinburgh by adding a chocolate ganache with a touch of good Scottish malt whisky complementing the traditional hazelnut praline. This is also an ideal pastry to serve at Easter time, as it could be dressed up to look like a nest. Over to your imagination!

1 Make choux dough as described on page 64 (except you are making a half quantity) or preferably use a half quantity of dough you have previously prepared. Pipe out the choux pastry in doughnut-sized circles about 8–10cm (3¼–4") in diameter using a plain or serrated 12–14mm (½") tip. Sprinkle with flaked almonds before baking for about 25 minutes at 160°C/320°F fan (Gas 4).

2 Make the hazelnut praline as described on page 171.

3 Gently heat the milk in a medium-sized saucepan with the coffee on low heat until nearly boiling.

4 Whisk the yolks and sugar in a bowl until light and creamy. Add the cornflour and continue to whisk until a smooth paste.

5 Pour half of the hot milk over the yolk mix, whisk, then add the rest of the mix to the saucepan, whisking constantly over a medium heat until the mixture thickens (about 5 minutes). Take off the heat and immediately cover with cling film to avoid a skin forming on the cream. Once cooled, transfer to the fridge and chill for at least an hour.

6 In a large bowl, cream the butter until light and fluffy. Whisk in the cooled cream and add the hazelnut praline. Leave to cool in the fridge for 10–15 minutes.

7 Break the chocolate into a bowl. Heat the cream and 1 tablespoon of whisky until nearly boiling, then pour half of it over the chocolate. Stir with a wooden spoon until melted then add the rest of the hot cream. Continue to stir until smooth. Add the other tablespoon of whisky. Leave to cool for 30 minutes (watch carefully that it doesn't harden too quickly if you put it in the fridge – otherwise add a bit more whisky!) then transfer to a piping bag with a plain tip.

8 Cut the choux circles in half horizontally with a bread knife.

9 Pipe out the praline filling on each bottom half using an 8–10mm (⅜") serrated tip then top with a line of chocolate-whisky ganache in the middle.

10 Place the tops on and dust with icing sugar. Chill until ready to serve the same day.

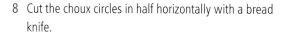

VARIATION

Mini praline choux puffs: Pipe out little choux balls (3cm/1¼"), top off with 3cm disks of craquelin (page 70) and bake for 15–20 minutes. Fill with the hazelnut praline and dust with icing sugar.

I made them for a party recently and a Frenchman came up to me in sheer disbelief, saying: "You made these – but how come? I heard you're Scottish." No comment.

7ème Arrt

RUE
DU
BAC

RUE
TARDIEU

18e Arrt

Salted Caramel Snowman

A NOT SO RELIGIOUS RELIGIEUSE

Makes 8 religieuses
Preparation time: I hour
Cooking time: I hour
Temperature: 160°C/320°F fan (Gas 4)
Bake large buns together (30 minutes)
   and smaller choux together (20 mins)

Choux dough:
150g water
100g milk
I tsp sea salt (or *fleur de sel*)
2 tbsps sugar
90g butter
150g flour (plain, all-purpose)
4 eggs

Salted caramel cream:
I x 2g sheet gelatine
100g sugar
100g cream, warmed
60g butter
½ tsp sea salt
150g mascarpone

Choux glaze:
2g gelatine (I x 2g sheet)
80g single cream
20g water
20g honey
120g white chocolate, broken into bits

Decoration:
8 small macarons (see page 106)
Mini Smarties ™
Mikado ™ chocolate sticks

Serve with Assam tea

The *pièce de résistance*, the *crème de la crème* of the choux, is the *religieuse*; but this is a not-quite-so-religieuse. It perhaps looks more fitting for a Mad Hatter's Tea Party but the kids love it. The best part is that it can be made using your leftovers. Each stage can be done separately in advance.

This treat is inspired by Christophe Roussel in **Rue Tardieu**, one of the most friendly, down-to-earth chocolatier-patissiers I know in Paris. He makes a salted caramel réligieuse with the traditional larger choux at the bottom, on a tartlet base, and a smaller choux placed on top, but either he tops it with a third mini choux or with a macaron. He calls it a *réligieuse qui n'est pas très catholique*, a French expression to say that something is a bit doubtful or worrying.

1 Make a choux dough following the instructions on page 64.

2 Using a piping bag with a plain tip (about 10mm/⅜"), pipe out eight large mounds of choux dough (about 5–6cm/2–2½" diameter) onto a baking sheet lined with either baking paper or a silicone mat. Bake in the oven at 160°C/320°F fan (Gas 4) for 30 minutes then leave to cool.

3 Make a second batch of choux buns but pipe out eight smaller heaps (about 2–3cm/1" diameter). Bake in the oven for 20 minutes.

4 Make the salted caramel mascarpone cream as described on page 159. Transfer the cream to a piping bag with a plain tip (ideally 6 or 7mm (¼"), small enough to pipe in to the bottom of the choux.) Now fill the choux buns. Making a small slit in the bottom of each, point the piping tip into each bun and pump in the pastry cream.

5 Make the glaze (see page 68) then dip the tops of the filled choux buns into it. Place small choux on top of the larger ones. Set aside to set.

6 Crown each religieuse with a macaron (page 106) and decorate with Mini Smarties ™ for buttons and eyes and with Mikado ™ chocolate stick arms.

Lime and Bitter Chocolate "Maclair" Tartlets

TARTELETTES CITRON VERT ET CHOCOLAT AMER

Makes 6
Preparation time: 1 hour
Cooking time: 35 minutes
Chilling time: 1 hour (minimum)
Temperature: 160°C/320°F fan (Gas 4)

6 leftover maclair chocolate macaron
  shells (from page 167) or:
60g ground almonds (almond flour)
90g icing sugar (confectioner's sugar)
50g egg whites
30g caster sugar (superfine sugar)
Brown powder or paste colouring

One portion of sweet, chocolate pastry
  (you'll only be using half):
125g butter, at room temperature
75g icing sugar
½ tsp salt
1 egg
½ tsp vanilla extract
240g plain flour (all-purpose), sifted
20g unsweetened cocoa powder

Lime cream:
Fine zest of 2 unwaxed limes
2–3 limes (100g juice)
125g butter, cut into bits
3 eggs
125g sugar
1 x 2g sheet of gelatine

Serve with Earl Grey tea

Inspiration for this tartlet came from tasting a simple, fluorescent green, domed chocolate in **Boulevard Saint Germain**, then **Place de la Madeleine** – marvelling at the eccentric giant chocolate chimpanzee and tiger sculptures, then again at the corner of **Rue Saint Sulpice**; all at the same *chocolatier*, Patrick Roger. It's here too that you can walk away with your chocolate in an emerald green handbag. It was perhaps a *petit* chocolate but the flavour was gigantic. The startling taste of lime and smooth, dark chocolate is sensational, waking up the taste buds. The fun part is adding a *"maclair"* shell (page 167) on top for a different texture. A toasted meringue topping is also mouth-watering.

1 Following the basic macaron recipe, pages 146–50, make chocolate macaron shells and pipe out long strips of about 10cm (4") as in the maclair recipe (page 167), or use your frozen leftovers.

2 Follow the basic sweet pastry recipe instructions, pages 106–9. Use a half portion (freeze the rest). Roll the pastry out to 3–5mm (⅛"–³⁄₁₆") thickness and cut out rectangles of about 12cm x 5cm (4¾" x 2"). Bake the rectangles in the oven at 160°C/320°F fan (Gas 4) for 15 minutes then set aside to cool.

3 Zest the limes using a microplane zester, a very fine grater (be careful not to grate the bitter white pith underneath too), and press out the lime juice, measuring to 100g.

4 Soak the gelatine in a bowl of cold water for 10 minutes. Put the zest, lime juice, butter, eggs and sugar in a small saucepan and mix gently over a low-medium heat until the mixture thickens. Take off the heat. Squeeze the gelatine of any excess water and mix into the lime cream. Transfer to a piping bag and leave to cool in the fridge for at least an hour.

5 Pipe out the lime cream on top of each chocolate pastry base and top with a chocolate maclair. Chill in the fridge until ready to serve.

My Opéra Éclair — Two Thirds Too Long

VARIATION ON A THEME

Makes 4 giant opera éclairs
Preparation time: 1 hour
Cooking time: 40 minutes
Chilling time: 2 hours
Temperature: 160°C/320°F fan (Gas 4)

Choux dough:

75g water
50g milk
1 tsp sea salt (or *fleur de sel*)
1 tbsp sugar
45g butter
75g flour (plain, all-purpose)
2 eggs

Chocolate coffee cream:
(overleaf)

Chocolate rectangles and stars:
(overleaf)

Coffee cream:
(overleaf)

Serve with Yunnan or Assam teas

I love opera and I love the classic opera cake but I find the opera recipe just a bit too long. With so many precise, pristine layers and complicated stages, it's a hard act to follow. To be honest, I prefer buying it, especially the reputed ones by Dalloyau on **Boulevard Beaumarchais**, opposite the Bastille Opera.

The opera cake changed the world of French pâtisserie, after its creation in 1955 by Cyriaque Gavillon, pastry chef at Dalloyau. This institution goes back to 1682 when Charles Dalloyau was official baker to King Louis XIV at Versailles.

Traditionally made with three slim rectangular layers of nutty *Joconde* cake, soaked in coffee syrup it's packed with sophisticated coffee cream, chocolate ganache and topped off with a chocolate glaze. The finale chorus finishes with a little gold leaf decor, just like the Opera Garnier's garnished roof, shimmering like a soprano's quivering vibrato.

Instead, I've made you a lazy gourmet éclair version, without losing the plot, and it's *Verdi* good. Like many pâtisseries do, a glaze is replaced with thin chocolate strips to decorate. Let's say it's a variation on a theme of an opera; and at about 25cm (10") after baking, it's an éclair two-thirds too long, topped off with an opera star.

If an opera éclair be the pastry of love, pipe on – to 17cm (7")!

1 For the choux pastry: Follow the basic recipe for choux pastry (page 64), except you are making a half quantity. Spoon into a piping bag with a 12mm (½") plain tip.

2 Pipe pastry to 17cm (7") in length onto a baking sheet covered in baking parchment or a silicone sheet. Leave plenty of room between the four éclairs.

3 Bake at 160°C/320°F fan (Gas 4) for 25–30 minutes till brown and crispy.

4 When cool, slice the tops of the giant éclairs completely off with a bread knife, ready for filling.

BOULEVARD BEAUMARCHAIS

Chocolate coffee cream:
200g milk
150g whipping cream
1 tbsp instant/soluble coffee
2 egg yolks
50g sugar
20g cornflour (cornstarch)
100g dark chocolate, broken into bits

Chocolate rectangles and stars:
50g dark chocolate
A chocolate transfer sheet

Coffee cream:
60g whipping cream
2 tbsps strong coffee (chilled)
40g sugar
125g (½ tub) mascarpone, chilled

5   **For the chocolate coffee cream:** Heat the milk, cream and coffee powder in a saucepan.

6   Meanwhile, whisk the yolks and sugar in a bowl until light and creamy. Add the cornflour and continue to whisk until smooth. Gradually add the warm cream and return it to the pan, whisking constantly over a medium heat until thickened.

7   Remove from the heat, whisk in the chocolate bits until melted into a smooth, luxurious cream. Set aside and chill in the fridge for at least an hour.

8   **For the chocolate rectangles and stars:** Melt 50g dark chocolate in a bowl over a pan of hot simmering water.

9   Using a transfer sheet with printed side up, spread on the melted chocolate using a palette knife.

10 Leave to cool in the fridge for 2 hours. Using a warmed knife (dipped in warmed water), cut out rectangles the same size as your giant éclairs, about 25cm x 4cm (10" x 1½").

11 If you have star-shaped cookie cutters, warm them slightly first before cutting out star shapes.

12 **For the coffee cream:** Using either a stand mixer or electric beater, whisk together the cream and coffee, then gradually add the chilled mascarpone until the cream is stiff.

13 Transfer to a piping bag with a serrated tip. Chill until needed.

14 **To assemble:** Generously fill the éclairs with the chocolate coffee cream. Discard the eclair pastry tops and instead top each éclair with a chocolate rectangle. Pipe on the coffee cream. Top with another chocolate rectangle. If you have an opera star then place it in the middle with some coffee cream for the final flourish.

Saint-Honoré with Violet

SAINT HONORÉ À LA VIOLETTE

Preparation time: 1 hour
Cooking time: 45 minutes
Makes 8

Choux dough (half portion of page 64):

75g water
50g milk
1 tsp sea salt (or *fleur de sel*)
1 tbsp sugar
45g butter
75g flour (plain, all-purpose)
2 eggs

Puff pastry:

250g ready-made, pure-butter puff pastry
(or ready rolled)
1 egg yolk (for glazing)

Mascarpone violet chantilly:

200g whipping cream (32–35%)
½ tsp vanilla extract
30g violet syrup (I use Monin's)
125g (½ tub) mascarpone, chilled

Caramel:

200g sugar
A little water

Serve with Darjeeling tea, or let's toast
Saint Honoré with a glass of chilled
Champagne or a Kir Royal, using Crémant
de Bourgogne with a touch of crème de
myrtille or blueberry liqueur

This final recipe has to be Paris's favourite special-occasion pastry.
Made in honour of Saint Honoré, the French patron saint of bakers
and pastry chefs, its name/saint's day (or *fête*) is on May 16. The
French are not huge on sending birthday cards but they always
make a point of saying "bonne fête" to someone on their name day:
possibly as it's easier to remember since it's marked on most French
calendars.

Just for the record, Saint Jill doesn't exist. For years I have confused the admin departments of French establishments. *Monsieur
Gilles Colonna* often appears on envelopes addressed to me. I don't
celebrate Saint Gilles' name day, however, since I'm not a man. I've
decided instead to celebrate in honour of bakers and pastry chefs
which is a guaranteed sweeter occasion.

Pastry Chef M. Chiboust, in 1847, created a pastry called the
Saint Honoré in his bakers shop in **Rue Saint Honoré**. With its puff
pastry circle as a base, a ring of choux pastry holds three little caramelised choux buns and traditionally topped off with a flourish of
crème chiboust (which is pastry cream with added egg whites and
gelatine), I've simplified it using a light mascarpone cream with a
hint of violet, which holds the pastry's hairdo just as well. Although
normally presented as round, you'll also find different Parisian chefs'
rectangular versions on display.

Don't be a shrinking violet. It perhaps looks like a complicated
challenge but the Saint Honoré just requires a bit of organisation.
You can buy the puff pastry and you can make the choux dough a
day or two in advance, the rest make the same day that it is being
eaten.

1   Preheat the oven to 160°C/320°F fan (Gas 4).

2   Using a cookie cutter of 10cm (4") diameter, cut out 8 discs of cold puff
    pastry and put onto a baking tray covered in baking paper or a silicone
    mat. Prick each disc with a fork.

3   You will need a half portion of choux dough (page 64).

4 Use a piping bag and a 10–12mm (½") plain tip to pipe out a ring of choux pastry, close to the edge of the puff pastry circle. Brush the choux and pastry edges with egg yolk. Bake for 30 minutes then cool on a rack.

5 On another lined baking tray, pipe out 24 (chouquette-size) heaps of choux dough. You will need three choux for each pastry. Bake for 15–20 minutes then leave to cool. Make the cream while the batches are baking.

6 Ensure the cream and mascarpone are chilled. Whip the cream, syrup and vanilla in a chilled bowl and gradually whisk in the chilled mascarpone.

7 Transfer the stiff cream to a piping bag with a 8–10mm (⅜") serrated tip (even better if you have a special Saint Honoré tip that makes waves) and chill until needed.

8 While everything is cooling and chilling, make a caramel to coat the choux puffs. Lay a sheet of baking paper on the counter. Heat 200g sugar in a saucepan with a few drops of water and over a medium heat, carefully watch it melt but don't stir. Put a folded, damp tea towel on the work surface. When the sugar has melted and starts to bubble, it will change colour quite quickly. As soon as it turns a goldenish brown, take off the heat immediately and place it on top of the tea towel.

CARAMEL

For the caramel to stay liquid while dipping in the choux, I make a slope with the tea-towel so that the pan is at an angle, keeping the caramel on one side of the pan. This will stop it from solidifying too quickly. If it does look like it's starting to harden quickly, transfer the caramel back to the heat for a few seconds and continue as before.

9 Dip each choux puff into the caramel (round side down) and place, caramel side down, on the baking paper to set.

10 To assemble them: Pipe out the cream in the centre of the disk. Place three caramel puffs on each disk (you could fill each puff with more cream but I just add more cream to the pastry, to be quicker). Pipe out the cream in between the puffs and decorate with blueberries and crystallised violets.

11 Chill in the fridge until ready to serve later in the day when still fresh.

CREAM

To whip the cream quickly, chill the bowl 30 minutes in advance.

VARIATIONS

Perfume the cream with syrups such as rose, cherry, strawberry, raspberry, lavender, praline, chocolate… over to your creativity. Why not make a "Macaronoré"? Replace the choux with three salted caramel macarons and replace the violet syrup with a good quality caramel syrup and some vanilla extract.

Appendix:
FAVOURITE SWEET WALKS IN PARIS

The following treasure hunt clues of pâtisserie locations is just a selection of some of my personal favourite places, either nearby or along your chosen route, just to give you a taste of Paris. Many of the names are already given in the recipes but there's not enough room to mention them all in a recipe book. I take no responsibility for whether you find yourself getting carried away and walking much further than planned. Just ensure you're wearing good walking shoes. Incidentally, many top *chocolatiers* make chocolate shoes, too. Which reminds me: bringing a cooler-bag around with you in the summer could be a good idea!

If you're in Paris for a long weekend, don't be surprised to see that most shops shut down on Sunday afternoons and Mondays. The good news is that there are still many fabulous pâtisseries that keep their doors open, especially nearer the areas with main attractions.

BANK TALK

Central Paris is divided in two by the river **Seine**: the **Left Bank**, south of the Seine (**Rive Gauche**) and the **Right Bank**, north of the river (**Rive Droite**).

Near the main tourist attractions, avoid the traps of expensive and nasty *menus touristiques*. Often just a 10–15 minute walk away there are some top-notch cafés, tea salons or pâtisserie boutiques where you can deliberate over your choice of a state-of-

the-art sweet treat to indulge in later by the Seine, a trickling fountain or on a shaded park bench while watching the world go by as you indulge.

NEAR THE EIFFEL TOWER
(LES INVALIDES AND RODIN MUSEUM)

If you're viewing the **Eiffel Tower** from the **Trocadero** end, then the **Place de Trocadero** has some good cafés if you become weary from taking photos of Paris's famous Iron Lady. For a pâtisserie of dreams with a tea salon, it's worth a ten-minute walk via **Avenue d'Eylau** to **Rue de Longchamp**. **Avenue Victor Hugo** is also a good address.

Nearer the Eiffel Tower itself – from the Ecole Militaire end, nearer Napoleon's tomb at **Les Invalides** – enjoy some chocolate and pastries from either side of **Avenue de la Motte Picquet** and enjoy a walk along by the lime blossom trees in the **Rodin**

Gardens. You're in the **7th Arrondissement** – home to some Ministries and Embassies. It spells elegance with apartment prices to match. Having lived in a

2–room box for five years in **Rue Bosquet**, I still love the ambience of the pedestrian street of **Rue Cler**. This has gradually become more touristic so head more into the side streets, such as **Rue du Champ de Mars** for a relaxing seat with some macarons and spicy hot chocolate. In **Rue Saint Dominique** there's a great variety of pastry boutiques, cafés, chocolate shops, a speciality canelé cake shop and a place where "everything's better" to stop for tea and chic

cakes. And if you're still looking for a cosy haven from the elements outside near the Eiffel Tower, head to a tearoom in **Rue de l'Université** where you're guaranteed two sugar "buzzes". In fine weather, there are plenty of crêpe and ice cream stands but walk to the corner of **Quai Branly** and **Rue de la Jean Rey** for a fun choux kiosk, owned by a star pastry chef.

Three blocks east of the Rodin Museum and you'll hit pâtisserie dreamland in **Rue du Bac**, which has a wealth of designer pâtisseries and signature chocolate shops (including tea salons). Finish off with La Grande Épicerie, the grandest gourmet grocery store in the **Rive Gauche (Rue du Bac/Rue de Sèvres)** and enjoy a break in the leafy park across the road.

NEAR NOTRE-DAME CATHEDRAL (ILE DE LA CITÉ)

This has to be one of the worst tourist trap areas where the coffees and treats are generally overpriced and not even great. Head next door to the **Île Saint-Louis** for an ice cream or hot chocolate and soak up the views and ambience of the River Seine, or head for some choux puffs in **Rue Galande**. Opposite the

Hôtel de Ville is a hidden tea salon haven on the 3rd floor of BHV with great views. If you have more time for pastries, head to **Saint Germain des Prés** first then return via the Bohemian Latin Quarter and enjoy your picnic under a Japanese cherry tree by the **Square Jean XXIII** next to **Notre-Dame Cathedral**. It's a favourite spot for brides when the blossoms are out in April.

SAINT GERMAIN DES PRÉS

This area (in the **6th Arrondissement**) is often nick-named the *quartier du chocolat*, since there are so many chocolate boutiques in such a concentrated area. **Saint Germain** is where art meets chocolate, pastry and macarons together and can be a tour in itself so, if you have a sweet tooth, then spend more time around here.

Starting in **Rue Bonaparte** (from the Seine side) with a couple of flagship pastry/macaron boutiques and a couple of chocolate boutiques, enjoy tasting their scrumptious specialities by the **Saint Sulpice Fountain**. This square is particularly pretty in Spring-time when the horse chestnut trees are in full bloom, resembling pink and white candles. Ah, the City of Light!

The real light comes from opening up your designer pastry "handbag": open it to marvel at glistening vanilla tartlets, rose, raspberry and lychee éclairs, Saint Honoré pastries or intriguing macaron flavours.

Look in the direction of the imposing Saint Sulpice church (complete with Delacroix frescos, made famous by *The Da Vinci Code…*) and enjoy the chocolate sculptures by an eccentric MOF (*Meilleur Ouvrier de France*) chocolatier who thinks outside the chocolate box. Head along **Rue Saint Sulpice** and **Rue Lobineau** (where there is an indoor market, great for cheeses) to **Rue de Seine**, one of my favourite addresses, home to one of the Parisians' favourite bakeries (their tea room is next door in **Rue des Quatre-Vents**), another MOF pastry boutique and a gifted chocolate maker who creates his chocolate bars (or "squares") from cacao beans himself. Across the **Boulevard Saint Germain**, pop into the historical cobbled passageway, **Cours de Commerce Saint André** for a hot chocolate and pastries and imagine every day is Sunday. A further walk towards the Seine to the charming 17th century square in **Rue Furstemberg** will not only take

you to the **Delacroix Museum** (this is a particularly arty area) but you should also take a breather with a few puffs of creamy choux, freshly filled in front of you.

If you're heading towards the Seine and **Pont-Neuf**, enjoy your treats seated under giant Catalpa trees in the **Square Gabriel-Pierné**.

For a longer picnic break, walk further to the end of **Rue Bonaparte** and enjoy your pastries in the relaxing and elegant **Luxemburg Gardens**. To add to your high-end picnic, discover contemporary Japanese-influenced French pastries nearby in **Rue Vaugirard** or more sumptuous chocolates around the corner in **Rue d'Assas**.

NEAR THE SACRÉ-COEUR BASILICA

The reputation around **Montmartre** or **South Pigalle** (SoPi) has radically changed since sex shops these days are gradually being replaced by "oh-la-la" pastry boutiques, many of them on **Rue des Martyrs**. In summer, head to the **Romantic Museum** in **Rue Chaptal** where you can enjoy a welcome tea stop in their leafy garden from March to October.

Nearer **Sacré-Coeur** admire the renovated **Abbesses** metro station opening, with its original 1912 Art Nouveau glassed roof. It's the deepest metro station in Paris, near the hill (*butte*) of Montmartre – as are mouth-watering chocolate *buttes* and kisses in **Rue Tardieu**, to help provide energy to walk up to the Basilica! At the top of the hill is the oldest building in Montmartre, now home to the **Montmartre Museum** in **Rue Cortot**.

NEAR THE PALAIS GARNIER (OPÉRA)

Just behind the opulent gold embellished Opéra are the *Grands Magasins* department stores on **Boulevard Hausseman**. Both of them have famous pastry houses and tea salons represented under one roof, although you may need to brave the crowds depending on the time of year you visit.

Walking by prestigious properties in **Rue de la Paix** towards **Place Vendôme** is like mentally playing the Paris Monopoly board game. This will lead you to a nearby hidden upstairs chocolate bar to your left at **N°231 Rue Saint Honoré**.

NEAR THE LOUVRE, MUSÉE D'ORSAY, TUILERIES GARDENS, CONCORDE, MADELEINE CHURCH

You'll find some hidden spots from the major touristy areas along **Rue de Rivoli** (opposite the **Tuileries Gardens**) where the queues for a Chocolat l'Africain in peak season may help you locate one of Paris' oldest tearooms! Head into **Rue de Castiglione** for an aristocratic dose of chocolate or to stock up on macarons in **Rue Cambon**. From **Place de la Concorde**, turn up **Rue Royale** for yet another historical tearoom which was originally a bakery in 1862, and where the

Parisian macaron was later created. If you don't want to wait for a table, marvel at the immense sculptures at the chocolate boutique in **Place de la Madeleine**. It's also home to two luxury gourmet stores at the back of the Madeleine church, which

have been there since the 1880s.

In the summer, **Les Berges de Seine** on the Left Bank (Rive Gauche) between the **Musée d'Orsay** and **Pont de l'Alma** has given way to pedestrians rather than traffic.

Take a stroll along the riverbank promenade, and set up your own pastry picnic at the *Terrasse à 1000 Pattes*, or even reserve time for an afternoon nap (*sieste*) by the **Port de Solférino** on weekends.

NEAR THE GRAND PALAIS AND ARC DE TRIOMPHE

The bottom end from the **Rond Point de Champs-Elysées (Clemenceau)** to **Concorde** is completely different to the more touristy top end towards the **Arc de Triomphe**.

If you're looking for quieter French tea-rooms with less of the queues, then enjoy them between the **Place de la Concorde** and south of Clemenceau under the shade of the horse-chestnut trees. However, one of my favourite exceptions on the **Avenue des Champs-Elysées** is further up at number 68. Just follow the scent of a little black dress down-

éclairs, pop into **Rue Pavée** en route or sit with a pot of tea (look out for the dormouse, or *loir*, in the teapot though!) around the corner in **Rue des Rosiers**, in the heart of the Jewish quarter.

If you have a longer stop, turn north to the **Upper Marais**. Destroy a delectable flaky millefeuille pastry at the top of **Rue de Turenne's** signature chocolate and pastry boutique's leather upholstered tea salon (which resembles more of a chocolate and pastry museum) or picnic on their exotic fruity caramels towards your next stop.

Continuing on **Rue des Francs Bourgeois**, pop in for some macarons with a Russian twist and sit like a Tsar in a Renaissance setting in the romantic little park, le **Jardin de l'hôtel Lamoignon**, on **Rue de Sevigné**. Otherwise continue on to the **Place des Vosges** and admire the square lined with elegant town houses. Either sit in the signature restaurant-tea salon or picnic in the central gardens and imagine Victor Hugo looking from his window at the duelling characters down below. He perhaps was inspired from this view but more pastry and chocolate views continue as our inspiration along **Rue du Pas de la Mule**.

stairs, which is disguised in the form of a fragrant chocolate-spiced and raspberry-tea-infused pastry. If you're splashing out, then there are also plenty of the top hotels in this area for a special occasion afternoon tea.

NEAR THE CENTRE POMPIDOU, PICASSO MUSEUM, PLACE DES VOSGES – THE MARAIS (4TH)

This area is so rich in museums, you'll definitely need to stop for the occasional sugar buzz.

From the **Pompidou Centre**, **Rue Rambuteau** has a couple of particularly excellent pastry boutiques: one of which specialises in mini "fairy" versions of the French classics and the other shouldn't be confused with a French lingerie underwear chain linked to sugared bread.

Continue along **Rue des Francs Bourgeois** towards **Place des Vosges**. If you fancy the latest

Ending up on **Boulevard Beaumarchais**, turn right and just opposite La Bastille's historic square, there's yet another opportunity to pop in for a reviving cup of tea over an opéra.

For those of you with a bit more time to spend in Paris, here are a few suggestions:

NEAR THE MUSÉE MARMOTTAN

Head out to the quieter, less touristic and residential **16th Arrondissement**. It's home to the **Marmottan Museum**, one of my favourite museums which is far smaller than Musée d'Orsay and a pleasure to visit for a couple of hours, where you'll see Monet's "Impression Sunrise" as well as his memorabilia and many more impressionist paintings. I worked around here for 10 years so should "know the area like my pocket", as the French say. The museum overlooks the **Jardin du Ranelagh**, (another creation of Baron Haussmann, who tidied up Paris into the long boulevards in 1871) a pleasantly tranquil picnic spot for some French-Japanese pastries from **Chaussée de la Muette** or creamy meringue marvels from **Rue de l'Annonciation** or éclairs from **Passy Plaza.**

If you are with smaller children, then the gardens have puppet shows in French (*les guignols*) and donkey rides. My favourite part during lunch hour was watching the hand-turning carousel from another era – children are encouraged to catch as many rings as they can with a wooden stick. Entertainment, indeed.

NEAR THE GREVIN WAX MUSEUM

Enjoy the glass and metal roofed passageway of the historical **Passage Jouffroy**, which not only hides one of my favourite, romantic tea salons with an extraordinary tea menu, but step back in time to 1845 when it was built and enjoy stylish window-shopping (or as the French say, *faire les lèches vitrines* – lick the windows). Continuing to the opposite end, turning left on **Rue du Faubourg Montmartre**, feast on marshmallows, chocolates, jellies at Paris' oldest confectionary shop, A la Mère de Famille, which started out as a little grocery here in 1761. Back to the passageway in the other direction towards the Grevin Wax Museum, the **Passage Jouffroy** is a continuation of the older **Passage des Panoramas**, built in 1800, across **Boulevard Montmartre**. Walk a bit further and you can stock up on your baking equipment in **Rue Montmartre**, so that you're ready to relive the recipe and Parisian pastry tour experience back home in your own kitchen.

BAKING EQUIPMENT
Some Essentials ... and Little Luxuries

Here's an overview of the tools you will need for many of the recipes. Some are not essential but are certainly useful to make baking life easier. **Rue Montmartre** (nearer the **Châtelet** end in the **1st arrondissement**) is the address in Paris for professional equipment and specialist baking ingredients, also conveniently open to the public.

BAKING SHEETS

Ideally, baking sheets (or trays) should be flat, so it's easy to slide your treats off the sheet (while still on the baking paper/parchment). It is useful to have at least three. When using silicone mats, I recommend placing them on baking sheets that have holes in them, which makes for a more even bake. A word on **baking paper/parchment**: good quality non-stick paper is essential for making macarons. I prefer using paper rather than silicone mats for macarons (for better feet) and there is no need to buy special moulded silicone macaron mats. On the other hand, for the rest of the recipes in this book, I recommend a plain silicone baking mat for pastries such as choux puffs, éclairs, millefeuilles, tuiles etc.

BALLOON (HAND) WHISK

A balloon whisk is essential for whipping up sauces and fillings to a smooth consistency.

BLOWTORCH

A culinary blowtorch is not essential, but it's a useful kitchen gadget to have if you're particularly fond of lemon meringue tarts or crème brûlées. If you don't have one, then place your preparation under a very hot grill (broiler) at 270°C/520°F for 3 minutes.

BOWL, SMALL METAL OR GLASS

A stainless steel or glass bowl is the ideal thing in which to whip up your egg whites, and it's handy for storing pastry cream in the fridge, covered with cling film. Glass bowls are good for melting chocolate gently over a pan of hot, simmering water (referred to as double boiler or *bain marie*).

CERAMIC BAKING BEANS

Baking beans are used for making larger tarts on top of baking paper, to stop the pastry from puffing up in the oven. If you don't find the ceramic beans in specialist baking shops, then just use dried haricot beans or even washed coins. Baking beans aren't needed for tartlets.

DIGITAL SCALES

Please don't start using this book without digital scales! If you don't have them already, this essential item (which is reasonably priced) will change your life in the kitchen. What's more, you can weigh your ingredients directly in the bowl or saucepan you're using, thus economising on washing up.

As baking in France is measured in grams, the recipes in this book are also given in grams. Baking by weight is far more consistent and reliable than baking by volume using cups – especially if you're baking macarons and pastries, where measurements need to be precise for the recipes to work.

If you're used to baking with ounces, it's

easy with a digital scale since most models have a button to enable you to simply switch from one unit to another.

DUSTER/SHAKER
Fill a sugar duster/shaker with icing sugar or cocoa powder and dust éclairs, cream puffs and fruit tartlets before serving. Why not also use a stencil to make patterns in icing sugar?

ELECTRIC WHISK
An electric whisk is essential for making macarons and meringues. An inexpensive, hand-held whisk does the job well, although if you have a free-standing mixer, even better.

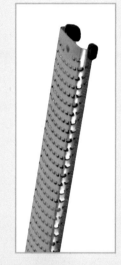

FOOD PROCESSOR
A food processor is not essential but takes the hassle out of crushing nuts for a praline, otherwise use a mortar and pestle.

MICROPLANE ZESTER
A Microplane zester is the best grater for zesting your citrus fruits. Remember not to zest the bitter white pith underneath.

MOULDS: NON-STICK TEFLON OR SILICONE
Non-stick moulds are easier to use since there's no need to grease and contents are easily removed. I recommend **eight tartlet moulds** (or inox rings) but some of the small cake recipes require the following particular moulds/pans (if you can't find them use muffin moulds):

- **Financier mould (oval 9 cavity** or use mini rectangular moulds, **25 cavity)**
- **Madeleine mould (9 cavity)**
- **Canelé mould (6 or 8 cavity)**
- **(Mini) savarin mould (18 cavity).**

OVEN THERMOMETER

Get to know your oven before you do anything (especially for baking macarons): your oven is your best friend. A good way of understanding your oven is to check that it's doing what it says it's doing by checking with an **oven thermometer** (available in all good baking stores). See page 19 for details on oven temperatures.

PANCAKE (CRÊPES) PAN

It sounds extravagant, but I have two small non-stick crêpe pans to make the pancake process so much quicker and easier – especially if you have hungry kids!

PASTRY RACK

A pastry rack or cooling rack is good for airing your cakes and choux puffs or éclairs. Also good for shaping *tuiles*!

PASTRY SCRAPER

A pâtisserie, or pastry, scraper is not essential for making macarons but I find it makes the process easier to produce a good, smooth batter. A scraper is also useful to push out batter or pastry cream from the piping bag, not leaving any waste.

PIPING BAG AND NOZZLES/TIPS

It may make baking sound pretty serious at first but, once you practise with a piping bag and nozzle a few times, piping batter can be an easy and quick process. An essential accessory for making macarons, it's also easy to pipe out dough or batter for choux buns, even for smaller teacakes such as financiers and madeleines. Disposable bags make life easy (even snip the corner of a sealed freezer bag) but, for those of you who bake often, I would suggest buying re-washable piping bags. It may seem expensive but if you bake cakes often, you'll see it's a great return on investment, especially if you buy 2 or 3 – also handy if you have leftover choux pastry dough and can leave it in the piping bag directly in the fridge for the next time and can still have another piping bag to hand for fillings.

Ensure you pick a bag (40cm/16") that has a loop at the top for hanging up to dry after cleaning. I have a **simple mini hook stuck to the kitchen window** to dry off piping bags quickly.

Don't forget the following nozzles or tips:

- ***Plain tip*** I generally use a 10–12mm (½") size tip. This is for piping out batter for macarons, mini cakes and small choux buns; 12–14mm (½–¾") is better for piping out éclairs.

- **Fluted/serrated tip**: 12–14mm (½–¾") for piping éclairs; 8–10mm (⅜") for wavy cream fillings such as the Paris-Brest or Saint-Honoré pastries.

- **To use a piping bag:** cut the bag at the extreme end and insert the tip. Fill the pastry bag, using a spatula or pastry scraper, about half (if you fill too much, it's difficult to control). Twist the bag around the top of the filling (you can clip the bag with a clothes peg or a bag closure until you gain confidence) and, using one hand at the base and one at the top, press down and push slightly from the top, releasing the filling.

ROLLING PIN

You need a decent rolling pin for uniform and thin tart bases; great for bashing speculoos biscuits too.

SIEVE

A sieve is necessary when making macarons to sift clumps from icing sugar and ensure the ground almonds are as fine as possible, but don't make your life a misery choosing a sieve with holes that are *too* small. Sifting almonds should only take 5 minutes maximum.

SILICONE BAKING MAT

Silicone baking mats are useful for baking choux buns, éclairs and tarts. Not to be confused with a moulded silicone macaron mat, which is not necessary for making macarons – you're better with good quality baking paper.

SILICONE PASTRY MAT (WITH DIAMETER GUIDE)

A pastry mat is not essential, but for making pastry for tarts, this is extremely useful and keeps your kitchen counter tidy.

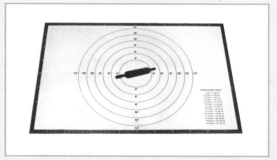

SPATULA

A good, flexible rubber spatula is essential for mixing with and makes a happy baker.

A metallic 38cm (15") spreading spatula, or palette knife, is used for covering cakes in ganache or icing (frosting). These can be straight or angled (cranked).

WOODEN SPOON

Last, but most certainly not least, a wooden spoon with a long handle is useful for preparing caramel, so that your hand isn't too near to boiling sugar projections. It's also useful for a "fanned" strawberry decoration technique (see page 120).

Picture opposite: Chocolate tartlet topped with chouquettes, page 180

QUICK REFERENCE GUIDE
FOR EGG WHITES

As you can't always predict the exact amount of egg whites you have saved up in making egg yolk recipes or saved up for macarons, here are some conversions for your macarons, financiers, tuiles and coconut macaroons. As a guide, one egg white is about 35g.

MACARONS

75g egg whites
40g caster sugar (superfine sugar)
90g ground almonds (almond flour)
125g icing sugar (confectioner's sugar)

60g egg whites
36g caster sugar
72g ground almonds
96g icing sugar

50g egg whites
30g caster sugar
60g ground almonds
90g icing sugar

FINANCIERS

100g egg whites
100g butter
86g ground almonds
100g icing sugar
36g flour
Pinch salt

70g egg whites
70g butter
60g ground almonds
70g icing sugar
25g flour
Pinch salt

TUILES

50g egg whites
50g caster sugar
23g plain flour
50g butter, melted
50g flaked almonds

MACAROONS

50g egg whites
85g desiccated coconut
60g sugar
2 tsps honey

STOCKISTS

FLAVOURINGS AND EXTRACTS

UK

thecakedecoratingcompany.co.uk

steenbergs.co.uk

vanillabazaar.com

vanillamart.co.uk

healthysupplies.co.uk

squires-shop.com

meilleurduchef.com

US

lorannoils.com

pastrychef.com

wilton.com

thevanillacompany.com

BOXES AND GIFT BAGS

UK

bagnboxman.co.uk

cakeboxesdirect.com

littleboxcompany.com

diyfavourboxes.co.uk

thefavourboxshop.co.uk

US

wilton.com

brpboxshop.com

CUTTERS AND STENCILS

UK

thecakedecoratingcompany.co.uk

almondart.com

cakecraftshop.co.uk

lindyscakes.co.uk

fmmsugarcraft.com

US

wilton.com

globalsugarart.com

COLOURING, EDIBLE LUSTRES

UK

cakecraftshop.co.uk

almondart.com

gold-gourmet.com

cake-stuff.com

partyanimalonline.com

houseofsugar.co.uk

windsorcakecraft.co.uk

US

uscakesupply.com

pastrychef.com

wilton.com

FRENCH BRANDS

UK

meilleurduchef.com

mondizen.com

frenchclick.co.uk

marketquarter.com

thegoodfoodnetwork.co.uk

macknade.com

US

thefrenchybee.com

saveurdujour.com

igourmet.com

FLAVOURED SYRUPS

UK

syrupsandstuff.co.uk

b-opie.com/pages/monin

monin.com

US

www.moninstore.com

BAKING EQUIPMENT, MOULDS, TRAYS

UK

kitchencraft.co.uk

johnlewis.com

ikea.com

nisbets.co.uk

procook.co.uk

lakeland.co.uk

amazon.co.uk

US

macys.com

thebakerskitchen.net

surlatable.com

amazon.com

CHOCOLATE

UK

willieschocolateshop.com

clarksfoodsonline.co.uk

chocolatetradingco.com

chocolate.co.uk

US

callebaut.com

chocoley.com

valrhona.com

chocosphere.com

STYROFOAM CONES AND OTHER SHAPES

UK

dummiesdirect.co.uk

US

hobbylobby.com

michaels.com

Acknowledgements
REMERCIEMENTS

A huge thank you to everyone who helped make this book possible – sticking by me on this fun, yet often daunting, adventure!

A special thanks to the team at Waverley Books for all your hard work, enthusiasm and support:— To Ron Grosset and Liz Small, for believing in me from the beginning and for making this next exciting project happen. To Eleanor Abraham, for her keen eye on recipe details, expert editing suggestions (including pun moderation), for ensuring a smooth layout, and for helping add to the collection with her lovely photographs of Paris. To Mark Mechan, for patiently wading through the hundreds of images, adding every stylish touch to make the book beautiful and still managing to keep an amazing sense of humour through thick and thin.

To Carol Gillott:— Thanks for stylishly putting my cakes on le map, the de-stressing lavender bags and cups of homemade cinnamon hot chocolate.

To Lily Heise at Context Paris:— Thanks for "convincing" me that to walk and talk pastries, macarons and chocolate was a great idea.

To my dearest family and friends:— A special thanks to Belinda Hopkinson and Emmanuelle Desreumaux. And to Antoine, Julie and Lucie, without your love, patience and encouragement I would never have arrived at this page.

To following friends on "Le Blog" for all your support and for sharing the passion.

Un grand merci to the many incredible pastry chefs in Paris who, through their constant temptations and wizardry, have totally inspired this Parisian journey.

Thank you!
Jill x

PICTURE CREDITS

Map illustrations courtesy of and copyright © Carol Gillott 2014.

Photographs by Jill Colonna, except for the following:—

Courtesy of Shutterstock:— Pages 20 (flour) © Viktor1; 23 (eggs) © goldnetz, (butter) © Alexander Dashewsky; 24 (chocolate), © Tim UR, (coffee powder) Bogdan Ionescu; 51 (Rue St Dominique) Alex Rodionov; 54 (Carousel) Anatoli Styf; 55 (Berthillon) © andersphoto; 122 (figs) © EQ Roy; 138 (Wild strawberry) © Natalila Melnychuk; 173 (bicycle race) © Radu Razvan; 211 (whisk) © M. Unal Ozmen; 212 (blow torch) © Jason Swalwell, (digital scales) © Pakawat Suwannaket, (baking beans) © area381, (bowl 1) © Ilya Akinshin, (bowl 2) © amphaiwan; 213 (madeleine mould) © Foodpictures, (zester) tacar, (food processor) © Sean van Tonder, (electric beaters) © PhotoBalance, (sugar shaker) © Theresa Scarbrough; 214 (scraper) © superdumb, (rack) © Mariontxa, (pan) © Angorius, (thermometer) © nui711; 215 (piping bag and nozzles) © M. Unal Ozmen; 216 (spoon) © ajt, (spatula 1) © VictorH11, (spatula 2) © Marc F Gutierrez, (silicone mat) © Michael Kraus, (sieve) © Africa Studio, (rolling pin) © sevenke.

Frames, courtesy of Shutterstock: pages 26 © Poprugin Aleksey, 62 © StudioZ, 104 © Ivan Smuk, 130 © NataLT, 142 © tawan, 178 © Chatchawan, 224 © Hein Nouwens.

Scrolls and flourishes throughout the book, the majority are courtesy of Shutterstock and © Woodhouse, except for (and repeats of) page 101 © Garry Killian.

Courtesy of Eleanor Abraham: pages 12 (patisserie), 14 (macarons), 15 (thé sign), 173 (bicycles, vélib), 189 (éclairs, millefeuilles).

Footsteps image by Mark Mechan.

Typeset in Bitstream Typo Upright, Bauer Bodoni and Humanist.

INDEX

First published 2015 by Waverley Books, an imprint of
The Gresham Publishing Company Ltd,
Academy Park, Building 4000, Gower Street,
Glasgow, G51 1PR, Scotland, UK.

www.waverley-books.co.uk

www.MadAboutMacarons.com

A catalogue entry for this book is available from the British Library.

978-1-84934-192-9

Printed and bound in China by WKT Company Limited.